Native American Studies

Native American Studies

Clara Sue Kidwell and Alan Velie

University of Nebraska Press
Lincoln

© 2005 by Clara Sue Kidwell and Alan Velie
First published in the UK by Edinburgh University Press, 2005
All rights reserved

∞

A CIP record for this book is available from the Library of Congress

ISBN-13: 978-0-8032-2776-7 (cloth : alk. paper)
          978-0-8032-7829-5 (pbk. : alk. paper)

ISBN-10: 0-8032-2776-0 (cloth : alk. paper)
          0-8032-7829-2 (pbk. : alk. paper)

Typeset in Monotype Ehrhardt
by Servis Filmsetting Ltd, Manchester, and
printed and bound in Malta

Contents

Acknowledgments (and apologies)

We acknowledge the vision of Robert Con Davis-Undiano, Neustadt professor of English at the University of Oklahoma and editor of the literary journal *World Literature Today*, in developing the Ethnic Studies series for Edinburgh University Press, of which this volume is a part. Jace Weaver and Jay Stauss read an early draft of the manuscript and made many helpful comments and suggestions. Jon Velie was of special assistance in the chapter on sovereignty.

We apologize to scholars whose work we have subsumed under the rubric of Native American Studies when perhaps they think it does not belong there. The attempt to trace the intellectual underpinnings of scholarship in a new field has led us to cast a wide net. We also apologize to those who feel that their work should be included but is not mentioned in this book. The scholarship on American Indians has grown at such a phenomenal rate – and is still growing even as this book goes to press – that it is impossible to mention all relevant publications.

Clara Sue Kidwell acknowledges an intellectual debt to colleagues and students in Native American Studies programs and institutions far too numerous to mention, but a few individuals deserve special thanks for thoughtful conversation and for fostering the intellectual environment out of which this book has grown. Jerome Greene, Ramon Powers, and Hoy Steele were steadfast colleagues in stressful times of change at Haskell Indian Junior College. Roger Buffalohead established the program at the University of Minnesota and gave me a chance to be part of it. Tim Dunnigan and Delores Cloud helped me understand the value of language, although I never mastered Ojibwa. Gerald Vizenor and Paula Gunn Allen at Berkeley challenged my thinking about literature. My faculty colleagues at the University of Oklahoma, Robert Warrior, Craig Womack, Geary Hobson, Loretta Fowler, Gus Palmer, Jr, Circe Sturm, Gary Anderson, R. Warren Metcalf, Al Hurtado, Josh Piker, Paula Conlon, Edgar Heap of Birds, and Mary Jo Watson, are doing the kind of scholarship that make Native American Studies such an exciting field. I was fortunate to be able to spend the 2003–4 academic year at the Newberry Library in Chicago, where Brian Hosmer, director of the D'Arcy McNickle Center for American Indian History, and Dan Cobb, assistant director, made me feel at home. I thank them and the Newberry staff for providing a supportive environment where I could finish work on this book. Finally, I owe special thanks to Vine Deloria, Jr, and W. Richard West, Jr. mentors in my short-lived museum career which has been such valuable experience in seeing things in new ways, as well as long-time friends.

Preface

The academic environment of a major university is alien to the experiences of most American Indians/Native Americans in the United States today.[1] Universities have, nevertheless, created programs devoted to the study of American Indian/Native American/indigenous peoples. These programs have taken many forms, from one or two courses in history or anthropology and some attention to special services and recruitment efforts for American Indian students, to the development of new courses and an academic curriculum specifically designated as American Indian or Native American Studies. Because such programs generally emerged from student activism in the late 1960s/early 1970s, they were suspect, and to some degree still remain suspect in the minds of college and university administrators as sources of political advocacy rather than academic objectivity.

Although many programs established in the enthusiasm of the 1970s have disappeared, other programs have survived and even thrived. They have led to new courses and new approaches to the study of American Indians. The development of the field has engendered the kind of intellectual debate that enriches any academic field. At its heart, the debate is an epistemological one. Should Native American Studies represent a distinct cultural viewpoint, and if so, how can it be understood by students from other cultures? If, as Calvin Martin asserts, Indian views of history are so distinctive from the concept of history inherent in Western European cultures, that non-Indians can never understand them, must we create a completely counter-historical narrative from a Native perspective?[2] Should Native scholars reject non-Indian scholarship altogether? And, given the historical experiences of American Indians, can the distinction between

Native and Western perspectives be so clearly made? The scholarship in the field of Native American/American Indian Studies has recently begun to address this last question in the form of studies that deal with the question of what constitutes Indian identity in contemporary society.[3]

In this book, we will argue that Native American/American Indian Studies programs are finding their voices within the academy because they have certain basic assumptions about the nature of knowledge. We will challenge traditional disciplinary divisions of knowledge within the academy and propose a new epistemology that emphasizes the interconnectedness of ideas about American Indians. We will explicate a set of assumptions that we think are essential to the field of Native American/American Indian Studies and that characterize the sometimes elusive notion of 'an American Indian perspective.'

The body of scholarship on Indians that has emerged in the fields of history, anthropology, and literature primarily since the late 1960s and early 1970s now provides the basis for critical analysis of what constitutes that perspective, and increasingly sophisticated methods of studying it. The interweaving of history and anthropology gives deeper insight into motives and causality in cross-cultural encounters. The exploration of social and political Indian identity in literature demonstrates the complexity of contemporary American Indian life beyond traditional stereotypes. At the same time, scholars in the field are debating a set of ethical standards for research that set out expectations with regard to the responsibility of Native researchers to Native communities. What obligation do they have to subject their research to the sanction and scrutiny of Native communities? Should they solicit their research topics from Native communities to meet the needs of those communities?[4] These questions raise the troubling question of who speaks for communities where factional disputes may pit members against each other. Issues of scholarly objectivity and political reality may well be at odds in these debates, but they contribute to the intellectual vitality of the field.

The approach we take is shaped by long experience in academic situations, and experience with Indian people in a variety of settings. We also draw on the scholarship of non-Indian authors, primarily historians, anthropologists, ethnographers, literary critics, and art historians, to demonstrate the extensive body of knowledge that has shaped American Indian Studies programs over the years. Although we argue that there are several premises that provide a coherent intellectual basis for Native American/American Indian Studies programs, we do not assert that they constitute the definitive statement of the field. One of the exciting things about our project is that Native American/American Indian Studies is a dynamic enterprise.

In presenting our critique of the field as an academic discipline, we hope to enhance its credibility in colleges and universities. By examining key premises of the field and the major intellectual issues that are the subject of debate within it, we try to make explicit what is meant by an American Indian perspective.

We hope that students in undergraduate classes, graduate students pursuing advanced degrees, and scholars who are established in the field will all find something of value in this book. Students may find useful information about the emergence of the field and its major scholarship. Established scholars may well challenge our premises and refine and expand them. In any event, we hope that the debate over our ideas will continue to enrich the field.

NOTES

1. In this book, we will use the terms interchangeably, since American Indian is still a legitimate historical term and is still widely used in many tribal communities. In Canada the term 'First Nations' is used, and increasingly the terms 'Indigenous' and 'Native' are used to indicate that Indians/Native Americans are the original inhabitants of the Americas. In terms of government policy, the first major piece of legislation to utilize the term Native American was the Native American Self-Determination and Educational Improvement Act of 1975. In 1978, Congress passed the American Indian Religious Freedom Act and the American Indian Child Welfare Act.

   In more recent years, the term 'indigenous nations' has sometimes been used in place of Native American. The University of Kansas, for instance, established an Indigenous Nations Studies master's degree program.

   In the academy 'Native American' is the term of choice, and academic programs are usually called 'Native American Studies' (NAS). Throughout Indian Country, on the reservation or off, Indians tend to refer to themselves as 'Indians,' or to identify themselves by tribal affiliation, or both.

2. Calvin Martin (ed.), *The American Indian and the Problem of History* (New York: Oxford University Press, 1987).

3. Circe Sturm, *Blood politics: Race, Culture, and Identity in the Cherokee Nation of Oklahoma* (Berkeley: University of California Press, 2002).

4. Devon A. Mihesuah (ed.), *Natives and Academics: Researching and Writing about American Indians* (Lincoln: University of Nebraska Press, 1998); Jace Weaver, *That the people Might Live: Native American Literatures and Native American Community* (Oxford and New York: Oxford University Press, 1997).

Native American Studies

CHAPTER I

Introduction

THE INTELLECTUAL BACKGROUND OF NATIVE AMERICAN STUDIES

Formal Native American/American Indian Studies programs are a relatively recent phenomenon in the academic world, and although their origins are usually associated with political activism, they have drawn from a strong American Indian intellectual tradition. In the early twentieth century, college-educated American Indians were speaking out on Indian rights issues, critiquing federal Indian policy, debating issues of American Indian identity, and seeking to preserve Indian cultures, all activities that generally characterize contemporary programs.

In 1913, the Society of American Indians was organized.[1] Among its leading figures was Charles Eastman, a Dartmouth-educated Dakota (Sioux) man whose writings about Dakota culture and history, published under his Dakota name Ohiyesa, became immediate best sellers.[2] Gertrude Bonnin, also Dakota, published under the name Zitkala-Sa.[3] Although their works were often classified as juvenile literature, they were read by adults as well. Carlos Montezuma, generally regarded as the most politically outspoken of the group, advocated the abolition of the Bureau of Indian Affairs and the full assimilation of American Indians into American society. His newspaper, *Wassaja*, published between 1916 and 1922, was his vehicle to inform audiences of Indian political issues.[4] Although the Society of American Indians largely ceased to function by the late 1920s, primarily because of the sharply divided opinions of its members on such issues as citizenship for American Indians and the role of the Bureau of Indian Affairs in Indian life, its existence is indication that the kinds of issues addressed in contemporary Native American/American Indian Studies programs are of long standing.

Native ethnographers contributed significantly to early development of the field of anthropology. George Hunt provided information and artifacts from the Kwakiutl tribe to Franz Boas; Francis LaFlesche worked with Alice Fletcher to document Omaha culture; and Arthur Parker (Seneca) was employed as an archaeologist by the New York State Museum and as an ethnologist by the New York State library. Parker served as president of the Society of American Indians in 1914–15. John N. B. Hewitt, a Tuscarora who was associated with the American Bureau of Ethnology at the Smithsonian Institution, published extensively on Iroquoian cultures. Ella Deloria (Lakota) is also recognized as an early ethnographer of her culture.[5] In some cases, contemporary communities are returning to these early ethnographic studies to recover information that has been lost to living memory.

In the fields of literature and history, during the 1930s D'Arcy McNickle (Flathead), wrote *The Surrounded*, a novel in which he expressed the angst of alienation from his own Salish culture when he went away to college, and John Joseph Mathews, an Oxford-educated Osage, documented the history of his tribe in *Wahkon-tan* and *The Osages: Children of the Middle Water*.[6]

The persistence of Indian cultures despite the policy of allotment of Indian land and cultural assimilation during the late nineteenth and early twentieth centuries led John Collier, Commissioner of Indian Affairs from 1934 to 1944, to promote their preservation through the Indian Arts and Crafts Act and the restoration of unallotted lands to federal trust status. The establishment of the National Congress of American Indians in 1944 fostered a new sense of political activism, and its executive director from 1964 to 1967, Vine Deloria, Jr, emerged as one of the leading Indian spokesmen and intellectuals of the twentieth century.[7] In 1961 the First Chicago Conference of American Indian Scholars brought together a group of intellectuals to begin to formulate a new political agenda for the mid-twentieth century.[8] In 1966–7, in an obscure journal called *New University Thought*, originating at the University of Chicago, Robert K. Thomas, a Cherokee anthropologist, published two articles that are considered seminal in the intellectual articulation of the position of American Indians politically in American society: 'Powerless Politics,' and 'Colonialism: Internal and Classic.' In these two articles Thomas placed Indian reservations as internal colonies in America and discussed strategies of resistance for Indian communities.

A new generation of Indian leaders emerged during the 1970s who had learned to deal directly with the political power structure of the Bureau of

Indian Affairs and of Congress. Although the American Indian Movement gained public attention for its violent and confrontational tactics, tribal leadership emerged in the figures of Mel Thom, Clyde Warrior (Ponca), Janet McCloud (Tulalip), and Ada Deer (Menominee), to name only a few.[9]

In 1972 the D'Arcy McNickle Center for the History of the American Indian was established under McNickle's direction at the Newberry Library in Chicago, and its seminars, fellowship programs, and scholarly resources contributed significantly to the scholarship on American Indian history that both enriched and was enriched by the establishment of American Indian/Native American Studies programs.

THE EMERGENCE OF NATIVE AMERICAN STUDIES IN THE ACADEMY

Native American Studies (NAS) programs are a relatively new phenomenon in academic institutions. They emerged in the intellectual and political ferment of the late 1960s and early 1970s, fostered significant new scholarship beginning in the 1970s, and have both contributed to and benefited from general trends in academic scholarship since that time.

In the 1960s and 1970s, civil rights and anti-war activism brought into sharp focus racist attitudes in American society, and the small numbers of students of all minority groups in colleges and universities were attributed to racist attitudes in those institutions. The very term 'American Indian' was politicized, some Indian activists seeing it as a European imposition on the native peoples of the Western hemisphere, a function of Christopher Columbus's confusion about his whereabouts in October 1492. The term 'Native American' soon began to replace it in US government documents and laws, although the usage was not consistent (see note 1 in Preface).

Student activism, including protests by white students, focused attention on the social inequity evident in the low numbers of Black, Chicano, and American Indian students on college campuses. College administrators could justify the establishment of academic programs that focused on specific racial/ethnic groups as a form of affirmative action. They assumed that such programs would be attractive to members of under-represented groups. American Indians had, of course, long been the subject of study in the academic discipline of anthropology. Vine Deloria, Jr, included a scathingly satiric chapter on the relationship between American Indians and anthropologists in his 1969 book *Custer Died for your Sins*.[10] Deloria's legitimate concern was that anthropological theories and studies were often driving forces in establishing federal policy. Indians also appeared in history textbooks, although to a great extent they conveniently disappeared almost immediately after European colonization.[11]

The challenge in developing the curricula of these new programs was to present a distinctive Native American perspective. More often than not, however, the strategy was to challenge stereotypes of Indians as hostile savages in the past or as drunken, poverty-stricken individuals in contemporary communities. The academic enterprise of presenting Indians as real people rather than stereotypes was part of the broader Civil Rights movement, which was played out not only in the political arena, but in cultural endeavors as well. The film *Little Big Man* (1970), a favorite among Indians, portrayed the Cheyenne Indians not as noble or bloodthirsty savages, but as complex human beings, which was ironically appropriate since the Cheyenne call themselves Tsitsitsas, which is literally translated as 'human beings.' Anti-war activists could also, however, see the attack on Old Lodge Skin's village (based on the historic massacre of Black Kettle's village on the Washita River in 1868) as metaphor for the massacre of Vietnamese villagers by US forces at My Lai in 1968.[12]

As the 1970s wore on, new images of Indians began to emerge in American society. Iron Eyes Cody shed a tear over the desecration of the environment in an expression of 1970s political sensibilities about pollution. In a tribute to the Indian occupation of Alcatraz Island in the San Francisco Bay area in 1969 and the violent confrontation of Lakota people and United States army forces at Wounded Knee in South Dakota in 1973, a poster began to circulate in Indian communities. Featuring a young Indian woman clad in buckskin, its caption was 'Better Red than Dead,' an ironic comment on the Cold War and anti-Communist hysteria in the 1950s.

While Indian activism led to physical confrontation and violence in the real world, most spectacularly the takeover of the South Dakota village of Wounded Knee in 1973 by members of the American Indian Movement, activism in the universities often involved reaction to existing academic assumptions as much as making a positive statement of Indian perspectives. Members of newly recruited American Indian faculties, expected to be both academics and activists, often found it necessary to counter traditional stereotypes and accepted truisms – for example, the 'virgin land' paradigm in American history – as well as to attempt to develop new ways of explicating knowledge about the nature of Indian life and the role of Indians in American history.

The texts available for Native American Studies classes were limited. Vine Deloria's witty critique of American perceptions of Indians, *Custer Died for your Sins*, took the academic disciplines of history and anthropology, as well as the whole American political and economic system, to task for the political oppression of Indian communities. Dee Brown's revisionist history of the west, *Bury My Heart at Wounded Knee*, exploited dramatic accounts of Indian massacres and battles to show why Indian responses were so violent.[13] *Black Elk Speaks, Being the Life Story of a Holy Man of the Oglala Sioux*, originally published in 1932 and reissued in 1961, soon came to be accepted as an authoritative statement of American Indian religious beliefs by progressive academics, New Age believers, and flower children who found it a source of a new spirituality.[14]

Although many academic administrators expected Native American/ American Indian Studies programs to disappear relatively quickly, and many indeed did, some, primarily those with a committed faculty, began to promote a new kind of scholarship that was more than a reaction to stereotypes. The University of Minnesota and the University of California at Berkeley emerged as leaders in the evolution of Native American/ American Indian programs. The program at Minnesota came out of negotiations between Indian students and certain key administrators who were sympathetic to their concerns. It thus enjoyed institutional support from the beginning.

The program at Berkeley emerged out of the violent confrontations between students and administrators that marked both the anti-war and civil rights movements of the era. When University administrators decided to cancel a scheduled speech by Black Panther spokesman Stokeley Carmichael, the resulting protest brought in not only black students but Hispanic, Asian, and American Indian students as well. As a result, the Chancellor and the Academic Senate agreed to the creation of an Ethnic Studies department that would answer directly to the Chancellor. Its position provided that the department would enjoy special protection, but it also cut it off from access to the usual processes by which academic programs were funded and staffed. Despite its anomalous position, the Ethnic Studies department survived and developed a strong curriculum.

A strength of the Minnesota curriculum was the inclusion of languages (Dakota and Ojibwe) as an essential part of the curriculum. The program could draw on Chippewa and Dakota communities in the state for Native speakers of the languages and trained linguists on its own faculty to structure teaching materials. At Berkeley, in the San Francisco Bay Area, a major center of urban relocation for Indian families in the 1950s, the curriculum emphasized contemporary issues. A course in tribal sovereignty was both a requirement and a guiding concept in the development of the program.

As programs established some sense of stability through the 1970s, a number of anthologies and new critical texts appeared, authored by both Indians and non-Indians. Geary Hobson's anthology *The Remembered Earth*, and Alan Velie's anthology *American Indian Literature* offered new access to Native literature. In the field of history, Francis Jennings's *The Invasion of America* provided a revisionist reading of colonial American history that examined the reasons for American Indian responses to European colonization and examined the attitudes of Europeans that inspired their often brutal treatment of Indians.[15]

These books are only three of the notable texts of the decade, which saw a virtual explosion of work in history and literature. In the field of anthropology, which had traditionally seen Native Americans as subjects, a new self-awareness of the role of researchers emerged. Jean Briggs's *Never in Anger* examined the influence of her presence in a Canadian Inuit community and her own responses to situations during her fieldwork.[16]

The new intellectual approach of cultural studies, which favored 'making the marginal central,' gave new latitude for American Indian scholars to develop their own ways of knowing. It was now fashionable to pay attention to the voices of those who had not been heard before. Biographies now became respectable academic sources of information for Native American Studies, not only those published as ethnographic studies (*Black Elk Speaks, Plenty-Coups, Pretty-Shield, Son of Old Man Hat, Dezba, Woman of the Desert*) but new works that reflected more contemporary sensibilities (*Half Breed* by Maria Campbell and *Lame Deer, Seeker of Visions*).[17]

In 1969, Kiowa author N. Scott Momaday's novel *House Made of Dawn* won the Pulitzer Prize.[18] The novel's troubled protagonist, Abel, was a veteran who was traumatized by his experiences in World War II, and ostracized by his tribe because of his illegitimacy. Ultimately Abel works through his difficulties and finds acceptance in his tribal community. Momaday's novel, a tour de force of powerful, poetic writing, initiated a scholarly interest in Native American literature and opened the way for other Native authors to publish their works in what became known as the American Indian Renaissance in literature.[19] Up until *House Made of Dawn* appeared in 1968, Indians had published only nine novels in the United States. Since then more than 200 have appeared. James Welch (Blackfeet) and Leslie Marmon Silko (Laguna) emerged not only as Indian authors but as major

American literary figures. Their works also laid the basis for the development of a critical stance toward the writings of Native American authors. Gerald Vizenor gained a reputation as an author with his novel, *Darkness in St Louis Bearheart*, and as a literary critic with the collection *Narrative Chance*.[20] A younger generation of authors emerged, most notably Louise Erdrich (Chippewa), whose *Love Medicine* won major literary awards in the 1980s, and Sherman Alexie (Spokane), whose novels and films brought him wide acclaim in the 1990s.[21] The works of these authors are now held as standards for Native literature. They have become accepted as subjects of study by graduate students and recognized scholars.[22]

ISSUES IN AMERICAN INDIAN STUDIES

The Canon

In any academic field, certain works have set standards for innovative approaches, have defined standards for critical analysis, or have become the subject of critique by scholars in the field of study. As American Indian Studies has entered the academy, the works of Deloria, Momaday, Erdrich et al. have become the staple of Native American Studies courses, but the question arose, should the field have a canon? Native scholars have challenged the canon of American literature, history, and the arts on political grounds, criticizing it as the work of 'dead white men' which ignores American Indian perspectives. If, however, a canon defines a common body of knowledge that a person must know in order to pursue further study of a field, then the works cited in this book constitute, in our opinion, a partial canon that has contributed to the intellectual development of the field of Native American Studies. Our choices are certainly subject to debate. The inclusion of new works in a canon, however, is a sign of vitality in the field, acknowledgement of the development of new critical standards and new approaches to research. Only when the canon becomes a static entity that suppresses new ideas does it cease to serve a useful role.

The canon of Native American Studies works is most extensive in the field of literature. Momaday, Silko, Welch, Erdrich et al. have produced works that have defined the field of American Indian literature. But Vine Deloria's *Custer Died for your Sins*, as a political statement, had a profound impact on American Indian activist movements in the 1970s, and his critique of the impact of Christianity on Native communities in *God is Red*

(1973) created a basis for dialogue and scholarship about the historical impact of Christianity on Indian communities.[23]

Local Knowledge and Global Knowledge

Another challenge to scholars in Native American Studies has been, if not to reconcile the local knowledge of Indian communities with the global knowledge paradigm of the academy, then to explicate the differences. Local knowledge constitutes the collective knowledge of a community. It is usually comprised of oral traditions, the collective memory of past events, and intimate knowledge of a particular environment. The academy, however, seeks global knowledge that can apply at all times in all places.

The academic disciplines which have used Indians as subjects of study – history, anthropology, religion, for instance – do not conform to the contours of Indian life. Oral histories that constitute part of the shared knowledge of a community, or even of a single family, do not necessarily agree in precise detail with written historical records. The oral histories can be seen as a counter-narrative to the Western historical tradition, and their failure to agree with positivist readings of the reality of the historical past does not automatically discredit them as useful information, alternative remembrances of the past.

Native categories of knowledge do not break out neatly as religion, philosophy, psychology, or history. Rather, they express relationships between people in different ways from the universal constructs that underlie traditional academic disciplines. The very term 'person' may well encompass humans, animals, rocks, rivers, and a myriad of other physical and spiritual beings who interact in complex ways. Anyone who has examined anthologies of American Indian literature finds chapters or sections that group stories into neat clusters, usually 'origin stories,' 'trickster stories,' 'stories of celestial phenomena,' or some other categorization that implies a set of absolutes.[24] The stories as printed are not, in the original versions, discrete units like Grimm's fairy tales. They are, rather, episodes within much longer sagas whose telling took hours and which wove together moral instruction, bawdy humor, fabulous adventures, and an explanation for why the world is the way it is. The nature of these tales defies the usual academic, linear logic that students expect in a classroom.

Published sources, which often betray the true nature of the original stories, complicate the task of explicating our premises. We must be concerned with processes and relationships rather than static and concrete facts. We must also appreciate the fact that these stories, in printed form, do not constitute an authoritative canon. One of the beauties of Indian traditions is their variability, the ways in which they fit themselves uniquely to places and peoples. We will deal with this point again in the section on language.

Finally, an essential premise of the local knowledge of specific communities is secrecy. On one level, the knowledge base defines the identity of the community, and refusal to share community knowledge with outsiders becomes a kind of protective mechanism to guard that identity, as ethnographers have sometimes learned to their frustration. Members of the Pueblo of San Juan in New Mexico, for instance, have objected to teaching their language to outsiders.

On another level, personal knowledge based on a relationship with spiritual beings cannot be available to all people within the group. Ceremonial initiation rites into secret societies or individual dreams and visions are sources of esoteric knowledge whose power depends on the fact that they are available only to selected individuals. If the power of generalization implies truth in the academic world, a sense of community or personal power means that certain kinds of Indian knowledge cannot be revealed.[25] This fact presents a significant epistemological challenge in teaching about American Indians.

The Native Perspective

Indians in the academic world often use the phrase 'a Native American (or American Indian) perspective' as a convenient short-hand term for the idea that Native Americans think differently from other people, but the phrase itself does not explain what that difference is. Rather, it smacks of essentialism, the concept of categorization that presupposes that people must think and act in certain ways because of their ethnic group or gender. Although N. Scott Momaday speaks eloquently of 'memory in the blood,' it is difficult to define the ineffable notion of Indianness. Given the extraordinary diversity of the indigenous tribes of the Americas, the number of distinct cultures and languages, the physical and genotypic differences, and the differing physical environments to which Indians adapted, it is impossible to speak of 'the' Indian. It is our challenge in this book to define what the uniqueness of American Indian perspectives is and to show how common themes and similar experiences have shaped the distinctiveness of American Indian identity.

Who is an Indian?

The question of who is an Indian is one fraught with biological, legal, and cultural dimensions, and there is no simple answer. Many Indian writers – Gerald Vizenor, Jace Weaver, Louis Owens, Geary Hobson – have engaged in debating what Weaver calls 'the gymnastics of authenticity' of Indian identity. One of the challenges of Native American Studies has been to explore the parameters of that identity in all its manifestations in contemporary society.

Discussions of Indian identity have to begin with 'blood.' The term 'blood' is of course unscientific – blood types are A, B, and O, not racial – but it it is so widespread in common parlance that it is impossible to avoid. Most Indians insist that claims to Indian identity must be grounded in some degree of blood quantum, some genetic tie to a particular tribe. In the eyes of the Indian community, it is not sufficient to wish oneself Indian. Although white Americans rarely claim to be Asian or Black, many have pretended to some quantum of Indian blood, enough people in fact that US Senator Ben Nighthorse Campbell, a Cheyenne, effected the passage of the Indian Arts and Crafts Act. This defines an Indian as a member of a federally recognized tribe, and has serious penalties (up to $250,000) for anyone who falsely sells something as 'Indian produced.'

But blood by itself is not enough. Most Chicanos have a substantial amount of Indian blood, more in fact than many Indians, but they have no cultural ties to American Indians, no legal standing as Indians, nor even a desire to be considered Indian. As Geary Hobson (Cherokee/Quapaw) has observed, 'While they are undeniably of Indian blood, and genetically Indian, they are nevertheless culturally and socially Spanish.'[26]

In legal terms, to claim Indian identity a person must be a member of a federally recognized tribe, and tribes have the right to recognize their own members as a function of their status as sovereign nations. Some tribes require a substantial blood quantum for membership: the Duckwater Shoshone require one half Shoshone blood; Mescalero Apaches require one fourth blood quantum. Many tribes, the Creeks and Cherokee, for example, require only that a member can trace his ancestry to a member on the original tribal rolls.[27] Tribes also have the right to adopt members, a choice that may not require any degree of Indian blood.

A person may be legally a member of a tribe, but not define himself as Indian culturally. That is, he or she may never participate in tribal rites or ceremonies, or acknowledge Indian identity in any way. Conversely, a person may define himself as an Indian, and have a substantial amount of

Indian 'blood' from one or more tribes, but if s/he is not enrolled in a tribe, s/he will not be eligible for federal benefits nor have the right to sell what s/he produces as Indian art.

Although sovereignty is an inherent right stemming from aboriginal occupation of the land by self-governing groups of people, the special political status of tribes in contemporary American society depends upon their acknowledgement by the US government. This relationship is political, not cultural, and the process of achieving federal recognition is a complex one encompassing seven major steps spelled out in the Federal Acknowledgement Act of 1978. Many tribal communities identify themselves, and may be recognized by outsiders based on cultural traditions and language and yet not be federally recognized. The Lumbee Indians in North Carolina have waged a campaign since the late nineteenth century to achieve recognition, and the Wampanoags of Mashpee, Cape Cod, were denied recognition despite substantial historical evidence in their favor.[28]

As Gerald Vizenor once commented, being an Indian in American society is a political act in and of itself. It is evidence of the failure of federal Indian policy to assimilate Indians into American society and of a tenacity of communities to cling to the ideals, values, and customs that make them who they are.

THE INTELLECTUAL PREMISES OF NATIVE AMERICAN STUDIES PROGRAMS

The intellectual premises that we set forth in this book emerge from these questions of what constitutes Indian identity in American society today. They are drawn from conversations with and writings by Native scholars, both within and outside the academy, and from personal experiences in Indian communities. They constitute a different epistemology for understanding Native people and Native communities in contemporary society.

The Significance of Land

The first of these is that Indian cultures arise from the relationship of people with the land on which they live. This is both simple and profoundly complex. The land, by which we mean the totality of the physical environment in which indigenous people live, is the ultimate source of spiritual power. By their relationships with the land, and its spiritual inhabitants, all people acquired the things that they needed for physical and intellectual survival. Humans categorized the beings of world around them and recognized differences among themselves, other groups, physical beings such as plants and animals, celestial phenomena, and intangible spiritual beings. They were concerned with maintaining harmonious relationships with all those beings. From those relationships spring the concepts that Western disciplines usually characterize as religion, anthropology, sociology, political science, psychology, and aesthetics. While these disciplines more or less take account of the influence of environmental factors in human societies, we argue that what makes Indians distinctive is that the relationship with the environment is the essential aspect of social organization and intellectual development.

Historical Agency

Our second premise is that Indians were active agents in, rather than the hapless victims of, forces of historical change. In the past, historians such as Francis Parkman and novelists like James Fennimore Cooper established the tradition of triumphalist narratives that glorified the advance of American society against backwards and dangerous indigenous peoples, while recent revisionist histories such as Dee Brown's *Bury My Heart at Wounded Knee* contributed to what Chippewa writer Gerald Vizenor calls 'victimist history,' laments about the plight of the poor Indian.[29] Most Americans are aware today of the one-sidedness and unfairness of treating history in terms of what Hollywood used to call 'the Winning of the West,' but the replacement for that, which sees Indians purely as victims, is often as bad. For centuries Indians were allies as well as enemies of whites in the Colonies and United States, and they gave as well as they got in battle. It is neither accurate historically nor fair to them to treat them as if they were nothing but hapless victims. Indians have much to be proud about in their history, and for whites to treat it as an unmitigated series of disasters is dishonest as well as condescending.

If treating Indians as hapless victims or bloodthirsty savages represents the extremes of interpretations of Indian-white relationships, the challenge for Native American Studies is to develop a more subtle and sophisticated understanding of the complexities of historical and cultural relations. A particular challenge in dealing with historical processes is that Indians did not have written languages in which to record their thoughts and deeds. Here the distinction between European and Native ways of knowing is very apparent in early contact situations if one can read behaviors rather than words. The study of behaviors has been the province of anthropology, but its application to an understanding of contact between European and Indian cultures has led to the emergence of the field of ethnohistory, which blends the synchronic approach of anthropology in describing culture as a specific set of behaviors with the diachronic study of history as a process of change.

Tribal Sovereignty

Our third premise is that American Indian tribes have the inherent right to be self-governing nations. That right, known as 'sovereignty,' stems from their aboriginal occupation of land and their processes of governing themselves. The relationship between the US government and American Indian tribes is a unique one, based on treaties signed with Indian nations as sovereign entities, and ratified by Supreme Court decisions like *Cherokee Nation v. the State of Georgia* (1831).[30] Although Indian nations have begun to reassert their sovereignty relatively recently in the mid to late twentieth century, today there are, essentially, three types of sovereign government in the US: federal, state, and tribal.[31]

In contemporary America, the federal/Indian relationship is defined as a trust, or fiduciary responsibility of the federal government toward Indian nations to manage their lands and resources for their benefit. The basic issue in the trust relationship today is who decides what is in the best interests of tribes: the US government or tribal people themselves?

The history of Indian-white contact shows the changing relationship between the tribes and colonial powers and then the United States, but the basic premise of treaty relationships remains a historical fact and is the basis of tribal sovereignty. The nature of the relationship has changed over time, from the initial dependency of European colonists on Indian people for physical survival, to US Supreme Court Justice John Marshall's decisions in the 1830s that defined the status of Indians vis à vis the US government as dependent, domestic nations, to an almost complete suppression of sovereignty under the assimilationist policies of the United States in the late nineteenth and early twentieth centuries, to the re-emergence of the concept of sovereignty in the 1960s and 1970s.

In the larger context of American history, tribal lands have become enclaves within the United States and particularly within state boundaries.[32] Relationships based on political power have changed. Indian tribes have been caught in the larger tension of states' rights versus the rights of the US government. Indian identity has assumed political dimensions that are intertwined with cultural ones. The study of this political relationship presents opportunities for a critical analysis of both American history and contemporary relationships between tribes and the US government.

The Significance of Language

Our fourth premise is that language is the main entrée into Native world views. The term 'world view' comes from anthropology, but it expresses the idea of a specific way of seeing oneself in relation to all other things in the environment. The issue of Native languages is both cultural and political in contemporary society. Language is essential to cultural understanding. And, for years it was a political issue in light of the federal government's historical policy of systematic suppression of languages in boarding schools for Indian students. That policy was repudiated by the US government in the late 1970s, but the damage was done when parents refused to teach their children their languages. Indian children continue to learn English exclusively in school, and the impact of television has speeded the loss of Native languages that continues and is a critical issue for contemporary communities. We will explore the nuances of world view in Indian languages and the issues of language retention in the face of historical pressure for Indians to assimilate into American society.

The Role of Aesthetics

The final premise is that art and aesthetics are essential ways in which contemporary Native people express their senses of identity. Again, this assertion seems obvious, but it encompasses the ideas of traditional images and relationships with the earth, the impact of historical change, and the notion of what constitutes Indian identity. At the heart of the discussion is the question of what constitutes a uniquely Indian aesthetic, which in turn raises the question of what constitutes Indian identity, and whether that question can be answered in any essential way. Is art done by American Indians, regardless of theme, American Indian art? Are all books written by American Indians to be studied as Native literature? In the study of aesthetics, these questions have led to the development of an academic stance of critical analysis. The creation of works of art and literature in a contemporary context has given rise to the question, 'how do artistic and literary works express American Indian values?'

CONCLUSION

As Native American/American Indian Studies programs have evolved in an academic context, they have moved from challenging stereotypes of American Indians in the popular imagination to grappling with complex issues of American Indian identity for individuals, and the political powers of American Indian nations as sovereign entities. As the relationship between federally recognized Indian tribes and the American government has evolved, those identity issues have become more complicated.

Native American/American Indian Studies has evolved as an academic discipline, both in the body of literature it has produced and in the sophistication of the questions it seeks to address. As the body of scholarship it has produced has increased, it has become more self-reflexive. This development is particularly marked in the field of literature, where the works of N. Scott Momaday, Leslie Marmon Silko, James Welch, Louise Erdrich, and Gerald Vizenor have become the subject of graduate student theses and dissertations in departments of English in major universities. In the traditional disciplines of history, anthropology, linguistics, archaeology, and others where scholarship on Indians still resides, interest in the study of Indians has grown. In specialized journals, scholars now have a forum.

Scholars who teach in Native American Studies programs are still largely trained in the disciplines of the academy – history, anthropology, literature, and the arts – where Indians have been seen as objects of study. Native American Studies scholars are still expected to fit their understanding of Native culture into disciplinary practices and perspectives. We hope that the following discussion of our premises will provide a framework for understanding the intellectual coherence of the field of Native American Studies and suggest ways to conceptualize new scholarship and develop new courses that will enrich existing programs in colleges and universities.

NOTES

1. Hazel W. Hertzberg, *The Search for an American Indian Identity; Modern Pan-Indian Movements* (Syracuse: Syracuse University Press, [1971]).
2. Charles Alexander Eastman, *Indian Boyhood* (New York: McClure, Phillips & Co., 1902); Charles Alexander Eastman, *From the Deep Woods to Civilization; Chapters in the Autobiography of an Indian* (Boston: Little Brown, and Company, 1916); Charles Alexander Eastman, *The Soul of the Indian; an Interpretation* (Boston, New York: Houghton Mifflin Company, 1911).

3. Zitkala-Sa, *American Indian Stories* (Washington: Hayworth Publishing House, 1921); Zitkala-Sa, *Old Indian Legends, Retold by Zitkala-Sa; with Illustrations by Angel De Cora Hinook-Mahiwi-Kilinaka* (Boston: London Ginn & Company, 1901).

4. Carlos Montezuma, *Let My People Go / Dr Montezuma Speaking in the Interest of his Race, the American Indians* (Chicago: Hawthorne Press, 1915).

5. Arthur C. Parker, *The Archaeological History of New York* (Albany, NY: The New York State Museum, 1922); Arthur C. Parker, *Indian Episodes in New York: A Drama-Story of the Empire State* (Rochester: Rochester Museum of Arts and Sciences, 1935); Deserontyon, John J. N. B. Hewitt, trans., *A Mohawk Form of Ritual of Condolence, 1782* (New York: Museum of the American Indian, Heye Foundation, 1928); J. N. B. Hewitt, *Iroquoian Cosmology* (New York: AMS Press, 1974, 1903: reprint of a work which was issued in two parts in the 21st (1899–1900) and 43rd (1925–6) annual reports of the Bureau of American Ethnology, Washington, DC, 1903 and 1928, respectively); Francis La Flesche, *The Osage and the Invisible World: from the Works of Francis La Flesche*, ed. Garrick A. Bailey (Norman: University of Oklahoma Press, 1995).

6. D'Arcy McNickle, *The Surrounded* (New York: Dodd, Mead, 1936); John Joseph Mathews, *Wah'kon-tah; the Osage and the White Man's Road* (Norman: University of Oklahoma Press, 1932); John Joseph Mathews, *The Osages, Children of the Middle Waters* (Norman: University of Oklahoma Press, [1961]).

7. Thomas Cowger, *The National Congress of American Indians: The Founding Years* (Lincoln: University of Nebraska Press, 1999).

8. Alvin Josephy, Jr, *Red Power: The American Indians' Fight for Freedom* (New York: American Heritage Press, 1971).

9. Robert A. Warrior and Paul Chaat Smith, *Like a Hurricane: The Indian Movement from Alcatraz to Wounded Knee* (New York: New Press, 1996); R. David Edmunds (ed.), *The New Warriors: Native American Leaders since 1900* (Lincoln: University of Nebraska Press, 2001).

10. Vine Deloria, Jr, *Custer Died for Your Sins* (London: Macmillan, 1969), pp. 78–100.

11. Frederick E. Hoxie, 'The Indians versus the textbooks: is there any way out?' *Perspectives: Newsletter of the American Historical Association*, 23, no. 4 (April 1985), 18–22.

12. Margo Kasden and Susan Tavernetti, 'Native Americans in a revisionist western; *Little Big Man*,' in *Hollywood's Indian: The Portrayal of the Native American in Film*, ed. Peter C. Rollins and John E. O'Connor (Lexington: The University Press of Kentucky, 1998), p. 125.

13. Dee Brown, *Bury My Heart at Wounded Knee: An Indian History of the American West* (New York: Holt, Rinehart and Winston, 1970).

14. *Black Elk Speaks: Being the Life Story of a Holy Man of the Oglala Sioux*, as told to John G. Neihardt (Lincoln: University of Nebraska Press, 1961).

15. Geary Hobson (ed.), *The Remembered Earth: An Anthology of Contemporary Native American Literature* (Albuquerque: Red Earth Press, 1979); Alan Velie (ed.), *American Indian Literature: an Anthology* (Norman: University of Oklahoma Press, 1979); Francis Jennings, *The Invasion of America* (Chapel Hill, NC: University of North Carolina Press, 1975).

16. Jean L. Briggs, *Never in Anger* (Cambridge, MA: Harvard University Press, 1970).

17. Maria Campbell, *Half Breed* (New York: Saturday Review Press, 1973); Frank B. Linderman, *Plenty-Coups: Chief of the Crows* (New York: The John Day Company, 1930); Frank B. Linderman, *Pretty-Shield: Medicine Woman of the Crows* (New York: The John Day Company, 1932); Gladys A. Reichard, *Dezba: Woman of the Desert* (New York: J. J. Augustin, 1939); *Son of Old Man Hat; A Navaho Autobiography*, recorded by Walter Dyk (New York: Harcourt Brace & Co., 1938); John (Fire) Lame Deer and Richard Erdoes, *Lame Deer, Seeker of Visions* (New York: Simon and Schuster, 1972).

18. N. Scott Momaday, *House Made of Dawn* (New York: Harper and Row, 1968).

19. Alan R. Velie, *Four American Indian Literary Masters: N. Scott Momaday, James Welch, Leslie Marmon Silko, and Gerald Vizenor* (Norman: University of Oklahoma Press, 1982); Kenneth Lincoln, *Native American Renaissance* (Berkeley: University of California Press, 1983).

20. Gerald Vizenor, *Darkness in St Louis Bearheart* (Saint Paul: Truck Press, 1978); Gerald Vizenor (ed.), *Narrative Chance: Postmodern Discourse on Native American Indian Literatures* (Albuquerque: University of New Mexico, 1989).

21. Louise Erdrich, *Love Medicine* (New York: Henry Holt and Co., 1984).

22. Arnold Krupat, *The Turn to the Native: Studies in Criticism and Culture* (Lincoln: University of Nebraska Press, 1996); Kimberly Blaeser, *Gerald Vizenor, Writing in the Oral Tradition* (Norman: University of Oklahoma Press, 1996).

23. Vine Deloria, Jr, *God is Red* (New York: Grossett & Dunlap, 1973).

24. Richard Erdoes and Alfonso Ortiz (eds), *American Indian Myths and Legends* (New York: Pantheon Books, 1984); Alice Marriott and Carol K. Rachlin, *American Indian Mythology* (New York: Thomas Y. Crowell Company, 1968).

25. Elizabeth A. Brandt, 'On secrecy and the control of knowledge: Taos Pueblo,' *Secrecy; A Cross-Cultural Perspective*, ed. Stanton K. Tefft (New York: Human Science Press, 1980).

26. Hobson (ed.), *The Remembered Earth* (Albuquerque: University of New Mexico Press, 1979), p. 10.

27. Russell Thornton, *American Indian Holocaust and Survival: A Population History Since 1492* (Norman: University of Oklahoma Press, 1987), pp. 190, 191.

28. Karen Blu, *The Lumbee Problem: The Making of an American Indian People* (Cambridge: Cambridge University Press, 1980); Jack Campisi, *The Mashpee Indians: Tribe on Trial* (Cambridge: Cambridge University Press, 1980).

29. See Hartwig Isernhagen, *Momaday, Vizenor, Armstrong* (Norman: University of Oklahoma Press, 1999), p. 85.

30. See Edward H. Spicer, *A Short History of the Indians of the United States* (Malabar, Florida: Krieger), p. 185.

31. See James J. Rawls, *Chief Red Fox is Dead: A History of Native Americans since 1945* (New York: Harcourt, 1996), p. 71.

32. Edward H. Spicer, 'European expansion and the enclavement of Southwestern Indians,' *The American Indian: Past and Present*, ed. Roger L. Nichols and George R. Adams (Waltham, MA: Xerox College Publishing, 1972).

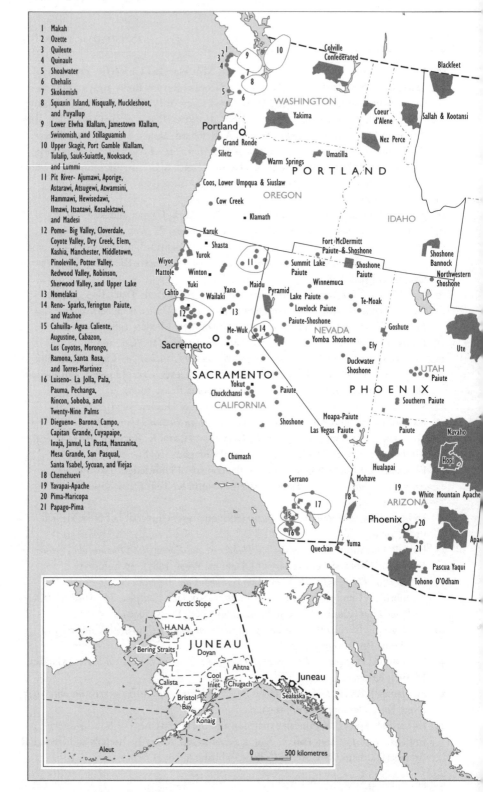

1 Makah
2 Ozette
3 Quileute
4 Quinault
5 Shoalwater
6 Chehalis
7 Skokomish
8 Squaxin Island, Nisqually, Muckleshoot,
  and Puyallup
9 Lower Elwha Klallam, Jamestown Klallam,
  Swinomish, and Stillaguamish
10 Upper Skagit, Port Gamble Klallam,
   Tulalip, Sauk-Suiattle, Nooksack,
   and Lummi
11 Pit River- Ajumawi, Aporige,
   Astarawi, Atsugewi, Atwamsini,
   Hammawi, Hewisedawi,
   Ilmawi, Itsatawi, Kosalektawi,
   and Madesi
12 Pomo- Big Valley, Cloverdale,
   Coyote Valley, Dry Creek, Elem,
   Kashia, Manchester, Middletown,
   Pinoleville, Potter Valley,
   Redwood Valley, Robinson,
   Sherwood Valley, and Upper Lake
13 Nomelakai
14 Reno- Sparks, Yerington Paiute,
   and Washoe
15 Cahuilla- Agua Caliente,
   Augustine, Cabazon,
   Los Coyotes, Morongo,
   Ramona, Santa Rosa,
   and Torres-Martinez
16 Luiseno- La Jolla, Pala,
   Pauma, Pechanga,
   Rincon, Soboba, and
   Twenty-Nine Palms
17 Diegueno- Barona, Campo,
   Capitan Grande, Cuyapaipe,
   Inaja, Jamul, La Posta, Manzanita,
   Mesa Grande, San Pasqual,
   Santa Ysabel, Sycuan, and Viejas
18 Chemehuevi
19 Yavapai-Apache
20 Pima-Maricopa
21 Papago-Pima

Indian Lands in the United States

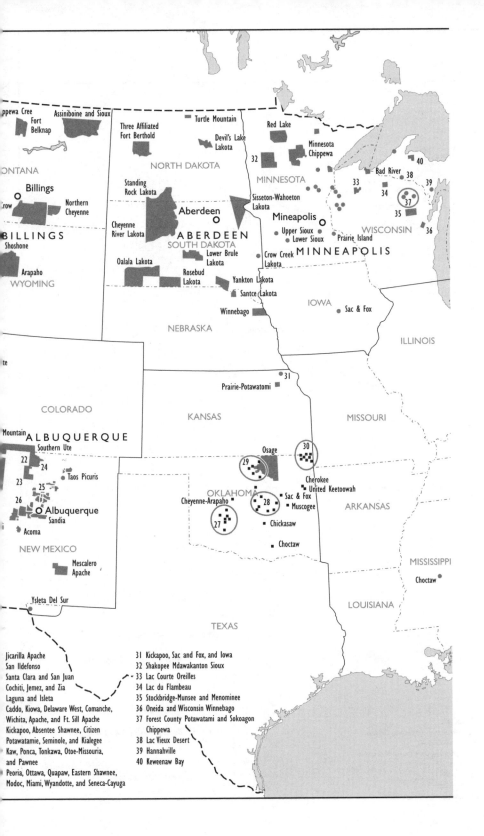

ppewa Cree
Fort
Belknap
Assiniboine and Sioux

Three Affiliated
Fort Berthold

Turtle Mountain

Red Lake

Devil's Lake
Lakota

32

Minnesota
Chippewa

Bad River

40

38

39

NORTH DAKOTA

MINNESOTA

33

34

37

ONTANA

Billings

row

Northern
Cheyenne

Standing
Rock Lakota

Sisseton-Wahoeton
Lakota

35

36

WISCONSIN

BILLINGS

Shoshone

Cheyenne
River Lakota

Aberdeen
O

ABERDEEN
SOUTH DAKOTA

Mineapolis
O

Upper Sioux
Lower Sioux

Prairie Island

MINNEAPOLIS

Arapaho

WYOMING

Oalala Lakota

Lower Brule
Lakota

Rosebud
Lakota

Crow Creek
Lakota

Yankton Lakota

Santce (Lakota

IOWA

Sac & Fox

Winnebago

NEBRASKA

ILLINOIS

te

31

COLORADO

KANSAS

Prairie-Potawatomi

MISSOURI

Mountain ALBUQUERQUE
Southern Ute

22

24

23

25

26

Taos Picuris

Albuquerque
Sandia

Acoma

29

Osage

30

Cherokee
United Keetoowah

NEW MEXICO

Mescalero
Apache

OKLAHOMA

Cheyenne-Arapaho

28

Sac & Fox

Muscogee

27

Chickasaw

ARKANSAS

Choctaw

MISSISSIPPI

Choctaw

Ysleta Del Sur

LOUISIANA

TEXAS

Jicarilla Apache
San Ildefonso
Santa Clara and San Juan
Cochiti, Jemez, and Zia
Laguna and Isleta
Caddo, Kiowa, Delaware West, Comanche,
Wichita, Apache, and Ft. Sill Apache
Kickapoo, Absentee Shawnee, Citizen
Potawatamie, Seminole, and Kialegee
Kaw, Ponca, Tonkawa, Otoe-Missouria,
and Pawnee
Peoria, Ottawa, Quapaw, Eastern Shawnee,
Modoc, Miami, Wyandotte, and Seneca-Cayuga

31 Kickapoo, Sac and Fox, and Iowa
32 Shakopee Mdawakanton Sioux
33 Lac Courte Oreilles
34 Lac du Flambeau
35 Stockbridge-Munsee and Menominee
36 Oneida and Wisconsin Winnebago
37 Forest County Potawatami and Sokoagon
   Chippewa
38 Lac Vieux Desert
39 Hannahville
40 Keweenaw Bay

Sault Ste Marie

41

42

43

MICHIGAN

Seneca

Onondaga

NEW YORK

Cayuga

MAINE

VERMONT

NEW HAMPSHIRE

MASSACHUSETTS

44

RHODE ISLAND

CONNECTICUT

PENNSYLVANIA

NEW JERSEY

OHIO

INDIANA

Washington

WASHINGTON D.C.

DELAWARE

MARYLAND

WEST VIRGINIA

VIRGINIA

KENTUCKY

NORTH CAROLINA

TENNESSEE

Eastern Cherokee

E A S T E R N

SOUTH CAROLINA

ALABAMA

GEORGIA

Choctaw

FLORIDA

45

46

	Federal Indian Reservation
– – –	Alaskan Regional Corporation
▲	State Reservation
▪	Federal Indian Groups Without Reservation
—— O	Bureau of Indian Affairs Area; Office

0   500 kilometres

41 Bay Mills
42 Grand Traverse Ottawa and Chippewa
43 Saginaw Chippewa
44 Narragansett, Mohegan, and Mashantucket
   Pequot
45 Seminole
46 Miccosukee

CHAPTER 2

Land and Identity

L and is the basic source of American Indian identity. Native people, who traditionally lived in subsistence cultures and drew the resources for their physical needs directly from the environment around them, saw themselves as causal agents in the processes of the world. Because their lives were lived in harmony with the cycles of the environment – the seasonal availability of food sources – they were aware that remembering what had happened in the past was predictive of what would happen in the future, but that their very thinking about the future had a causal effect. Ceremonial activity became a way of physically renewing the world. Ways of knowing about the world involved both learning social sanctions through ceremonial activities, stories and place names, and acquiring individual abilities and understandings through personal experiences such as dreams, visions, and initiation rites. These experiences were necessary to establish appropriate senses of relationship with the non-human beings of the world, and the maintenance of social harmony among the members of the group and beneficial relations with the forces of the physical environment – that is, the non-human world – required knowledge of appropriate and respectful behavior.

The extent to which this idealized sense of Native American world views persists in contemporary communities is, of course, one of the major issues that underlies the discussion of Native American identity that we have initiated. Given the historical changes that have occurred since the time of European contact, the majority of Native people now live in urban environments rather than in reservation communities. Most who are employed participate in American society as wage laborers rather than subsistence farmers. Christianity has become an important influence in both urban and reservation communities, although it is impossible to give any statistically accurate count of American Indians claiming church membership. Christian Indians may actively disavow ceremonies and former beliefs as pagan, but they may also worship with hymns sung in their Native languages (often the only vestige of Native language use in a community). Tribal governments, however, identify with the tribal land base as a source of political power, and in urban communities Indian people very often identify themselves by who their families are and what reservations they came from. Native languages are generally being lost, and much of ceremonial life based on traditional usages of a land base has either disappeared or is expressed in much modified form from earlier practices. It is, of course, impossible to know for certain the forms that communal cultural practices are taking in Native communities at any particular point in time, but tribal memory is a powerful force, and it can keep alive the knowledge of how things have been done.

We argue, therefore, that knowledge and understanding of the association of one's ancestors with a particular homeland is an essential part of a Native American Studies curriculum. The source of American Indian identity is, as it has always been, their association with the land on which they live. The notion of land encompasses earth and the sky, the physical phenomena of lakes, rivers, oceans, the totality of flora and fauna, rocks and mountains. The environment is the physical manifestation of spirituality. The natural world within which Indian people live is filled with beings – many of which whites would consider inanimate, such as rocks and hills – who are sentient and wilful. It is also the source of tribal memory. The red rock formations scattered in the northern section of the Navajo reservation are the remains of the monsters slain by Child of Waters and Monster Slayer. The great monolith in Wyoming named by the National Park Service as Devil's Tower is the refuge where seven Kiowa sisters took refuge when their brother turned into a bear. The Black Hills in South Dakota rose where the land was pushed up as the two leggeds (the Lakota people, the birds and the bears) and the four leggeds (all the other creatures) pounded down the land during their great race.[1]

This assertion about the relationship of land and spirituality means, in the beginning, that we must realize the seemingly capricious actions of the natural environment – storms, drought, the actions of the hunter's prey – as evidence of will and volition, qualities seen in both human and non-human beings, animals, natural phenomena, and spirits. We must also realize that the environment in all its aspects holds richly symbolic meaning. The idea of Corn Mothers prevalent in Pueblo societies, for example, creates an association between the power of women to give birth and the fertility of the land in the growth of crops.

The Cherokee story of Kanuti the Hunter and Selu the Corn Mother defines the roles of men and women in relationship to their environments. Kanuti kept the animals in a cave and had only to release one in order to kill it for food for his family. His two sons, however, curious about the source of their food, followed him and opened the gate to the cave, allowing the animals to escape. Henceforth, men must hunt the animals for food. Selu fed her family a delicious food, but she would not reveal its source. The sons, again curious about how she acquired it, followed her one day and discovered her rubbing skin from her body into a basket. The skin became the grains of food. When she saw that they had discovered her secret, she told them that they must kill her and drag her body seven times around the ground that surrounded their cabin. They killed her, but they were lazy and only dragged her once, and then not over the whole area before they buried her. The next spring, corn grew from the earth where her blood had touched the ground, but it only grew once a year, and only in certain places.[2]

The story of Selu embodies the complex ways in which seasonal cycles in agricultural societies mirror the larger cycles of human life. Selu must die so that the corn can be born. The corn plants must grow, only to be cut down in the harvest. The warmth and rain of summer must give way to the killing cold of winter before the cycle can be repeated. So human cycles of birth and death go on. Death is not an end in itself, merely a necessary part of life. Time is cyclical, not linear.

The relationship of American Indian societies to land is also essential to the process of historical adaptation and change. In contemporary America, it is basic to political issues of tribal sovereignty. In rural reservation communities that do not have many of the material advantages of American mainstream life, for example in communities where unemployment levels are high and family incomes are low, the land still provides elements of basic subsistence in hunting or gardening and reinforces the cyclical nature of time. For those who have moved off the reservation, the chance to periodically come back to tribal lands provides spiritual sustenance.

The concept of spirituality in the natural world may seem strange to those raised in one of the world religions like Judaism or Christianity that for the most part developed in urban environments. These religions depended upon specialization of social roles, centralization of control over resources, and the control of spiritual knowledge by a priestly class.

Exodus tells us that the Hebrews were forced to wander in the wilderness, which was a threatening rather than an enlightening experience. The religion was manifest in the tablets of the Ten Commandments, a statement of religious dogma, housed in the Ark of the Covenant, which was portable so it could accompany a wandering people. The Promised Land was in the settled territory of the Canaanites, so Joshua fought the battle of Jericho, a walled city, to claim the security of urban settlement for the Hebrews.[3] The city of Jerusalem became the central site of Judaism with the construction of the temple that housed the Ark. Christianity arose in the urban environment of Jerusalem and flourished in Rome as a religion of the proletariat. Islam arose as the religion of tribal people, but it soon centered on urban areas such as Mecca, still a source of religious pilgrimage. Buddhist temples make Kyoto in Japan a religious site. Although these sites are important to their religions, these religions place more importance on events than places, and they put ultimate importance on the continuation of human existence in some world beyond the present. As Vine Deloria, Jr, explains:

> The vast majority of Indian tribal religions . . . have a sacred center at a particular place, be it a river, a mountain, a plateau, valley, or other natural feature. This center enables the people to look out along the four dimensions and locate their lands, to relate all historical events with the confines of this particular land, and to accept responsibility for it . . . Other religions also have a sense of sacred places. The Holy Land has historically been a battlefield of three world religions, each of which has particular sacred places it cherishes. But these places are appreciated primarily for their historical significance and do not provide the sense of permanency and rootedness that the Indian sacred places represent.[4]

ORIGINS

American Indian stories of the origin of the world orient people to the land, in all its aspects, and to the sky. Stories of tribal origins give people their sense of place in the world. They are not stories of the creation of a world *de novo* but ways of establishing human relationships with existing environments. They may, for purposes of discussion, be grouped into two broad categories, origins in the sky, and origins below the earth.

The World Above

One great intellectual achievement of American Indians was to understand the cycles of the stars and seasons. They recognized not only the obvious diurnal movement of the sun, but its movement across the horizon from solstice point to solstice point, and its relationship in the sky to the moon and stars and planets. The earth is the microcosm of the sky, the vast macrocosm above. The relationship with the sky is apparent in the Iroquois tradition in which a woman fell through a hole in the world above. This world was covered with water, but the birds caught the woman as she fell, and a turtle rose from the water so the birds could set the woman down on its back.[5] The turtle's back became the earth. The term 'Turtle Island' is often used in contemporary tribal statements as a metaphor for the earth's surface as a home for human beings. The Hopi in the southwest observed not only the monthly waxing and waning of the moon, but also the more complex relationship of the movements of the sun and moon in relation to each other.[6] The Pawnee on the central plains recognized the movement of the planets with relation to the fixed stars. They explained their origin as a people by the relationship of the Morning Star and the Evening Star, whose union produced the first woman, and they oriented their villages with relationship to patterns in the stars.[7]

Medicine wheels, circles of stones or wooden posts laid out on the landscape were permanent markers of solstice points, which indicated the change of seasons. The medicine wheel in the Big Horn Mountains of Wyoming marks solstices but may also have marked the helical rising of the bright stars Rigel, Sirius, and Aldbaran, giving predictive indicators of the amount of time remaining until the next solstice.[8] Tribes generally marked solstice points to help with planting seasons, but the hunting tribes of the Big Horn Mountains used them as well. For many tribes, the first appearance of the Pleiades in the fall marked the end of the agricultural season.[9] The Lakota in the northern plains explained the Pleiades as seven young girls who were stolen by an eagle and killed. A Lakota warrior finally killed the eagle and put the girls' spirits in the sky. Certain events in Lakota history were associated with the spirits of the girls, and Lakota holy men still make pilgrimages through the Black Hills to a series of sites that commemorate those events and follow the movement of the Pleiades across the night sky.[10]

Knowledge of these cycles was not the work of a single individual, or of a single generation. It depended on systematic observation over long periods of time. The very process of systematic observation gave form to native ways of thinking. According to Francis LaFlesche, the Osages originally 'kept together for protection and moved about without tribal or clan organization,' but finally

> a group of men fell into the habit of gathering together . . . to exchange ideas concerning the actions of the sun, moon, and stars which they observed move within the sky with marvelous precision, each in its own given path . . . from one side of the sky to the other without making any disturbances in their relative positions, and that with the great movements four changes take in the vegetal life of the earth, which they agreed was affected by the actions of some of the heavenly travelers.[11]

These men noted a 'procreative relationship' between the earth and celestial bodies, and a 'silent, invisible creative power' Wa-kon-da, as the source of all being.[12]

The World Below

Other stories involve an emergence from a world below, often but not always followed by a migration to a specific place. The Tewa Pueblo story of how the people came to the Middle Place begins with an emergence from a series of worlds below this. Grandmother Spider was at the place of emergence to give advice about where the people were to live and a warning of what would happen if they went beyond the bounds of their land. The cold in the north, the searing heat of the sun in the south, the threat of hostile tribes in the west, all serve to define the land on which the Tewa lived, and beyond which to go was dangerous. When those who had ventured beyond the boundaries were killed, one boy and one girl were left, and they became the progenitors of the tribe. Grandmother Spider gave them a sign of where they should be when they saw a turtle, whose shell carried the design of the spider's web.[13]

The Present World

Origin stories give a spiritual sanction to people's occupancy of their home lands. They provide a sense of the boundedness of place. In villages, human community is carefully structured by kinship relations and sense of obligation and responsibility. The world beyond the village, the organized space of society, is the realm of spirits, and it is dangerous to those who do not have the knowledge to protect themselves in encounters with spirits. In this respect, origin stories serve to reinforce moral values of respect for teaching of the elders and the power of knowledge. The present Chippewa world was created after the first was covered by a great flood. The otter finally dove to the bottom of the water and brought up a small bit of mud that Wenebojo, a spiritual being, blew on four times, and it expanded into a new earth.[14]

A Lakota (Sioux) story tells about the origin of the Black Hills. The two leggeds (humans, birds, and bears) and the four-leggeds agreed to a race that would establish who had the power to kill whom. They lined up and began running. They ran so fast and so long that they wore down the race track, pushing up the land in the center (the Black Hills). As they finally reached the finish line, the buffalo was in the lead, but the magpie, which had perched on his hump throughout the race, calmly rose and flew over the line ahead of him. The two leggeds won the race and claimed the right to use the four leggeds for food, but they also agreed to treat them with respect.[15]

PLACE, SPACE AND TIME

The markers of time – that is, the movements of the sun, moon, and stars, the growth of crops, the harvest – repeat themselves in predictable cycles. People know what has gone before, and they anticipate what will happen in the future. Their expectations are met to a greater or lesser degree in each new seasonal cycle. In their thinking about the future and hoping for the fulfillment of their desires, they become causal agents in the processes of nature. Anticipating future events based on memories of what occurred in the past becomes a way of understanding the processes of the world.[16]

This notion of the creative power of human thought is exemplified in Pueblo societies in the figure of Tch se nako, or Thought Woman. She is the creative force who thinks things into existence. She has two beings, Ursete and Naosete, who make her thoughts manifest.[17] People participate through ceremonies in which human energy is essential to the continuance of seasonal cycles.

This idea that human beings are, indeed, causal agents in shaping their environments derives from the sense of place in Indian societies. They act both in the physical labor that they expend to hunt animals, to prepare skins for shelter and clothing, to clear fields, to plant, cultivate, and harvest, and also in the ceremonies that establish the relationships with the spiritual beings who are the ultimate source of what people need. Pueblo communities of the southwest have a yearly cycle of ceremonies. Alfonso Ortiz has described the ceremonial cycle of the San Juan Pueblo in the 1970s. Each of the eight ceremonial societies have specific periods during the year in which they pray and fast. Their ceremonies also presage the events that are expected, for example the 'Bringing the Buds to Life Ceremony' occurs in February.[18]

The cyclical nature of time means that people have the power to renew the places in which they live. The 'world renewal' ceremonies among the tribes of California emphasize the importance of place, of renewing one's world through one's own efforts on an on-going basis. The ceremonial activity involves moving from place to place, reciting the stories of events that have occurred at certain places, ritually stomping the earth to firm it – events that meld physical earth and human activity into a seamless whole.[19]

The Pawnee Morning Star Ceremony celebrated the power of the earth to produce corn and women to produce new life. A young girl captured from another tribe was given the best food and clothing before she was killed and buried face down in the prairie. She represented the first woman, offspring of the stars, and her body and blood returned to the earth as a source of the creation of new life, the corn that the Pawnee cultivated.[20]

WAYS OF KNOWING

The key to understanding the power of the environment for Indians is to understand the sense of awe that they experience in their encounters with the forces of nature. It is a profoundly personal and emotional response to the unknown, and it serves to create a sense of personal relationship between humans and spirits. The nature of this relationship may be understood in an intellectual way, but the specific nature of the personal relationship is beyond ken. It is essentially knowable only to the individual. There is ultimately no way that one person can have complete knowledge of another's visionary or dream experience with the spiritual forces in the environment.

Dreams, vision quests, and initiation rites are all ways Indians acquire knowledge of and relationships with the spiritual forces of nature. Dreams, in their symbolic aspects, the way they express the fluidity of time, and the way that dreamers can commune with dead relatives, are a different form of reality, but to Indians they are every bit as real as the waking world. In particular, dreams in which the dead appear provide proof of the idea of immortality.[21]

A Chippewa woman said once that 'People who can't dream are like people . . . who can't read.' Dreams are powerful tools for understanding the world. She explained that she had had a dream of horses, and thereafter people were always giving her horses.

Dreams are also ways of understanding the relationship between humans and animals, hunters and their prey. A Pawnee story tells of Small, an orphan boy who fell asleep by the river one day while hunting ducks. He awoke in the ducks' lodge under the river, where they were sitting in council to decide his fate. Should they kill him, as he intended to kill them, or should they take pity on him? They agreed that although he hunted them, they decided to allow themselves to be killed as food, and thus, they allowed him to live and to hunt them.[22]

Seeking visions is a more active way than dreaming of gaining knowledge and establishing relationships. Vision quests must be understood in terms of the dichotomy between the constructed world of human society and the natural realm of spiritual power. Many Native people still believe that individuals have dreams or visions that give them special abilities, such as curing, or controlling weather, or special skill in hunting.

Outside of the social world, however, the spirits in the natural world have their own societies, and particular powers. An Indian who seeks a vision must go outside the village to encounter the spirits on their own terms. The practice of vision seeking still goes on for Indian men in some communities. It has enjoyed a resurgence among Lakota and Cheyenne communities on the Great Plains. Lakota men go to certain places in the Black Hills. High places are important because they are places where the powers of sky and wind intersect with the powers of rocks and earth and beings who move on the earth. Vision seekers abstain from sexual intercourse, and they take sweat baths to cleanse themselves of human smell. They shed their clothing. They fast, depriving themselves of food. They strip themselves of everything that they can of the human world to prepare themselves to encounter the spirits.[23]

The encounter occurs when a spirit manifests itself, most often in its animal form, although sometimes it is only a voice that would give instructions or teach a song. The spiritual being might leave a tangible sign, such as a feather, a rock, or some other distinctive object. Whatever the experience, it is a life-changing one, from which a man emerges with a new sense of his relationship to a particular spirit and a sense of his ability to perform certain deeds because of that relationship.

Although in the older forms of vision seeking the exact nature of the visionary experience could not be known by others, there was always some behavioral change that manifested itself in the individual to demonstrate that he did, indeed, have some new power or understanding. In contemporary society, where men generally cannot pursue the traditional activities of hunting and warfare that allowed a man to demonstrate his newfound powers, the issue of behavioral change is of less importance than formerly.

In a particularly dramatic historical account of power, Roman Nose, a Cheyenne warrior, was prohibited by his spiritual guide from eating meat touched by iron. Before the Battle of Beecher's Island in 1868, an encounter with the US Army, he ate with one of his fellow warriors, and his host's wife, unbeknownst to him, lifted the meat from the cooking pot with an iron fork. Until then Roman Nose had been able to ride into enemy fire without being harmed. When he discovered that his power had been broken, he declared that he could not fight the next day. When his followers said that they could not be successful without him, he finally agreed to fight, but he predicted his own death. He was killed by a bullet that struck him in the side.[24]

Plenty-Coups, a Crow leader in the late nineteenth century, described his dream of a storm knocking down a forest. Only one tree was left standing, and at the top of the tree was the nest of a small chickadee. The chickadee became Plenty-Coups's helper. Its ability to listen quietly gave Plenty-Coups his ability to listen to the debate in councils, to reflect all that he had heard, and to give wise advice.[25]

Initiation into a secret society is yet another way of gaining knowledge. The Hopi spiritual beings known as kachinas, for instance, live in their world below, which is a mirror image of this one. During the Pueblo growing season, the kachinas' world is cold and dark, and they come to spend their time in the world above. When the growing season in this world has ended and the harvest has been completed, the kachina world is coming to life, and they must return to plant and harvest their crops. Kachinas who first appear in the villages in the fall become part of the community's life. Hopis teach that bad children may be carried away into the forest to be eaten. During certain ceremonies kachinas may appear at the doorways of the homes of unruly children, and only offerings by their parents save them from being devoured.[26]

For the Hopi, imitating kachinas on earth is an important part of ceremonial life. During certain ceremonies relatives take children into the kivas,
the underground ceremonial chambers, where the kachinas beat them with
yucca whips, which often draw blood. The kachinas then divest themselves
of their masks to reveal that they are male relatives. Don Talayesva (Hopi),
describes the way he was initially disillusioned, but reflects that ultimately
he developed an understanding of his relationship with the kachinas. He
realized that the men who donned the masks did so to allow the kachinas to
embody themselves so they could interact with the Hopi. The men assumed
a responsibility to the kachinas, and the kachinas came to ensure that the
Hopi people would have what they needed from the environment in order
to survive.[27]

Power and Knowledge

The world of nature is one of power. To many Indians winds, plants,
animals, even rocks may be sentient beings, and their power can be harmful
to those who do not understand and know how to use it. Spiritual power can
be compared to electricity. Ordered through knowledge (that is, in wires and
circuits), electricity can be directed into useful work. In nature, in the form
of lightning, it can do tremendous harm.

Power is a pervasive presence in the world. The Chippewa term
'manitou', the Lakota term 'wakan tanka', and the Iroquois word 'orenda'
are all expressions of this sense of power. This power manifests itself in
physical phenomena. A Lakota man in the late nineteenth century
described a pantheon of sixteen deities, including the sun, the moon, the
blue of the sky, and the four winds from the four directions of the world,
which are all manifestations of the power of wakan. This notion of manifestation of spirituality in physical phenomena is essential to understanding Lakota culture.[28] It is also analogous, however, to the Christian mystery
of the holy trinity. For the Lakota, winds, rocks, celestial bodies, the buffalo
are all manifestations of the ultimate reality of wakan. Each element has its
particular importance in Lakota life. The sixteen physical manifestations
of spiritual power for the Lakota parallel the three elements of the
Christian trinity, the Father, the Son and the Holy Ghost, which embody
specific intellectual and emotional aspects of Christian dogma. In both
systems, the singularity of emanant spiritual power manifests itself in
many things.[29]

THE AMBIGUITY OF POWER: THE TRICKSTER AND THE CLOWN

The world is an uncertain place. Physical phenomena are capricious; they produce beneficial and harmful effects in the lives of human beings. Rain causes crops to grow but can also cause floods. An individual can achieve a relationship with spiritual forces, but because it is so personal, there is no universal contract for a standard result, as there is in Christianity and Islam. Nor is there a concept of good and evil in the Christian sense. Christians are more likely than believers in traditional Indian religions to think of people as either righteous or depraved. And, Indians did not traditionally view spiritual forces as either inherently benevolent or malign, as Christians do.

The ambiguity of power is embodied in the figures of the trickster and the sacred clown,[30] as illustrated in a story about Wenebojo, the Chippewa trickster. Wenebojo kills the Snake King to avenge the death of his nephew Wolf. The Snake King's death throes raise the great flood that submerges the world (snakes being associated with water). Having caused a disaster, Wenebojo must find a way to fix things, which he does by sending various animals to dive below the waters to bring up earth again. He is thus both a destructive and creative force in one being.[31]

Tricksters take different forms in different tribes, but whether they take the form of animals or humans, they display a range of behaviors, sometimes acting as creators, sometimes as buffoons.[32] Saynday pulls the Kiowas through the hollow log from the world below to this earth, and he brings the Kiowas the sun which was captive on the other side of the earth.[33] But he also gets himself stuck in a buffalo skull, and is badly battered when he tries to have sex with the Whirlwind.[34] Wakdjunkaga, the Winnebago trickster, almost drowns in his own feces when he eats a laxative, but he also kills the evil beings that menaced the Winnebago in their homeland.[35]

The trickster as a creative force defines people's complex relationship with the world around them. With his insatiable appetites, Wenebojo regularly kills and eats his animal relatives – another commentary on human-animal relations. The environment both nurtures and threatens, and the trickster dances on the boundary between sustenance and destruction. The trickster embodies both the wilfulness of nature and the extremes of human behavior. He is ultimately selfish, a creature of enormous physical appetites – always ravenously hungry, sexually predatory, and greedy for what others have – but he is also easily tricked and often the buffoon in situations with humans and other animals. He is constantly on the move, 'going along,' as the ritual formula has it, from place to place, seldom part of a settled community. He rarely accepts responsibilities. His selfishness means, however, that he is totally gullible, easily tricked into self-destructive behavior, unable to see the consequences of his own actions. He is the ultimate figure of mutability and changeability in the world.

Coyote is the most common trickster figure among Indian tribes. In nature the coyote (the animal, not the trickster) is the ultimate survivor, an animal that has spread its territory from Los Angeles to New Jersey, while its cousin the wolf is all but extinct. In the western states today, coyote hides often adorn fences as trophies. In a sense, they demonstrate Coyote's most remarkable trait. He is always getting himself killed, yet he is still always there. In a contemporary story, Coyote, in a fit of generosity, gives his good Pendleton blanket to a rock on a cold day. As the weather gets progressively worse, however, he decides to take it back. The rock will not part with it willingly, so Coyote grabs it and wraps himself up. He soon hears a rumbling noise in the forest and sees the rock rolling toward him. His attempt to flee is futile as the rock flattens trees, rolls through rivers, and ultimately squashes Coyote flat in the road. A rancher, driving by in his pick-up, decides that the hide will make a good rug and takes it home and puts it in front of the fireplace. Coyote, however, comes back to life, puffs himself up, and runs away, upon which the rancher's wife remarks at breakfast that 'I saw your rug down the road this morning.'[36]

Coyote's greed, foolishness, and sexuality are not cause for ultimate damnation, but rather part of the cycles of nature and human existence. He does not stop to judge the consequences of his behavior, but stories about him teach people to do so. Coyote stories are always humorous, but ultimately moral. They teach that moderation and self-control are the important values in society, that greed is destructive, and that individuals have different qualities and abilities that must be respected.

HUMOR AND THE SACRED

There is a deep connection between the sacred and the humorous, as demonstrated by the Sacred Clowns, who play an important role in ceremonies in many cultures. Clowns may be seen as a reification of the trickster of tribal story, brought to life in tribal ceremony. It is useful to consider Mircea Eliade's definition of the sacred as a form of 'ontological separation' from ordinary life.

It is important to bring out this notion of peculiarity conferred by an unusual or abnormal experience, for, properly considered, singularization as such depends upon the very dialectic of the sacred. The most elementary hierophanies, that is, are nothing but a radical ontological separation of some object from the surrounding cosmic zone; some tree, some stone, some place, by the mere fact that it reveals that it is sacred, that it has been, as it were, 'chosen' as the receptacle for a manifestation of the sacred, is thereby ontologically separated from all other stones, trees, places, and occupies a different, a supernatural plane.[37]

For example, the association of humor and sacredness comes in the break between expected and the unexpected that inspires a person to stop and consider the nature of reality, and to come to new understandings of the world. The anthropologist A. Irving Hallowell asked an Ojibwe man 'Are all the rocks we see around us alive?' The man pondered a minute, and then replied 'No, but some are.' Hallowell was seeking a generalizable linguist principle to distinguish animate and inanimate categories in the Ojibwe language, but we must consider, with Hallowell, what distinguishes 'some?' Hallowell learned that some stones were observed to move of their own accord, so to speak, to fall unexpectedly down chimneys into fireplaces.

The unexpected behavior, the ontological break in the physical world, marked certain rocks as spiritual beings. Hallowell's ethnographic inquiry, Eliade's theoretical statement of the ontological separation that characterizes the sacred, and the Ojibwe man's straightforward account of his experience, create a context for the idea that understanding different ways of knowing is implicit in Native American Studies, and these different ways are critical to understanding how cultures may interact.

Humor, in the form of the Sacred Clown, may be defined as the juxtaposition of the unexpected, and it constitutes a similar disruption of the ordinary. The image of the flattened Coyote as a rug that runs away is funny because of its unexpectedness. Humor is, however, a very serious part of ceremonial activities. Sacred clowns in Pueblo societies parody the order of the world, and their disordering of the normal course of human affairs creates a space where spiritual power may enter the human world. Don Talayesva described how he and his fellow clowns performed mock sexual intercourse with a clown dressed as a woman in the plaza at Old Oraibi. When he directed his fellows to bring wood to build a house, they brought ashes.[38]

Power is, however, dangerous. The humor of clowns expresses disorder, and disorder is dangerous. Its unpredictability makes it powerful. The unexpected happens. In some ceremonies, clowns smear themselves with feces and drink urine to demonstrate their impunity to social norms. They also mock and ridicule behaviors that are socially unacceptable, a powerful form of social control. They inspire feelings of shame. The Koyemci, or Mudhead clowns in Zuni society, are the offspring of an incestuous relationship between a brother and sister. Their ludicrous antics in ceremonies stem from the shame of their birth, and reinforce norms of sexual behavior.[39] The clowns are sacred because in the context of the ceremony, they are part of the disordered world, yet they suffer no consequences because of their actions. Rather, they remind their audience that disorder is dangerous because it is not under human control.

Although clowns flout convention, they are not punished. Like tricksters, clowns teach moral lessons. By holding up actions to ridicule, they teach what is acceptable behavior. Laughter becomes a way of enforcing moral values in society. It also, as Black Elk said in regard to the Heyokas, men who did everything backward, opened the mind so that people would understand the sacredness of the world.[40]

THE MORAL IMPLICATIONS OF THE LAND

The landscape also holds moral implications. Events that occurred in certain places long ago have meaning for contemporary Indian societies. A series of Western Apache stories show what happens when people do not follow social values of reciprocity and appropriate ceremonial behavior. For example, at one place, aptly named Shades of Shit, some people who refused to share their corn with their relatives, whose crops were poor, were forced to remain in their homes (shades) by their relatives and had to live in their own excrement. They became sick and nearly died. The place and its name thus remind people of what happens when they become greedy and do not share with those who are in need.[41]

Relationships in tribal communities throughout the world serve the ends of basic human survival, that is, cooperation and reciprocity. When humans depend on the environment for food and shelter, they must work together because the individual is unable to survive alone. How individuals work together leads to a myriad of ways of organizing societies, and the patterns of organization in American Indian societies demonstrate that complexity.

A basic premise of social organization is that groups of individuals must have a leader. A second premise is that men and women are different. These differences give rise to the ultimate cooperation in human society. Versions of the Navajo origin story, for example, posit Father Sky as a great impregnating force, with his clouds and rain, lying over Mother Earth. Their union produces life. Part of the Navajo origin tradition tells what happened when men and women separated. The women went across the river, and for the first year they gave birth to children, but then they ceased to have babies and the crops that they planted failed, and they began to satisfy their sexual urges with plants and animals and gave birth to monstrous beings. Finally, they gathered on the river bank to tell the men that they wanted to come back, and the men agreed. The moral of the story, if one may call it that, is that men and women belong together.[42]

Another principle of social organization is that there is a spectrum of values in Indian societies, from a premium on individual exploits to an emphasis on communal action, that is again dependent on people's relationship with the land, and their ways of subsistence. On the plains, the relationship between men and buffalo was paramount. The Lakota story of how men had established their right to kill buffalos in the great race between the two leggeds and the four leggeds explained how, when men provided food for their families through hunting, they could attract women. Men must, however, prove their abilities, and they did so through the spiritual sanction of their visions, which must be demonstrated in their skill in hunting and their bravery in battle. The women's tremelo (a high-pitched, wavering cry) signaled their approval of men's actions. Men adopted markers of their individual exploits: headdresses, shirts trimmed with enemy scalps, and war shields adorned with images that signified their visionary powers.[43]

The Pueblos represent the communalism in Indian societies, although their diversity shows a range of values. The contemporary western Pueblos, the Zuni, Hopi, Acoma, and Laguna, were (and to a large extent, are) dry farmers, that is, they relied on rainfall to grow their crops. Families tended small plots that were subject to the vagaries of the seasonal and brief rains that swept across the landscape. It took careful planning to capture this rainfall to nurture the corn. Family members had to work together on their farms. The pueblo communities along the Rio Grande river drew water from it to irrigate larger areas of land. The larger fields needed more collective labor. They divided into halves (moieties) rather than family units.

Marriage between men and women is necessary to procreation. It also provides the mechanism by which human societies share their resources. Marriage is not primarily a matter of sexual desire. Coyote stories teach that lesson. As Black Elk commented about High Horse, whose love of a woman drove him to desperate deeds when her father would not let him marry her, love is a sickness, not the basis for making a lifelong alliance. It drives people to do irrational things, but they will ultimately recover their senses.[44] As men and women share resources in marriage, their union involves the resources of the larger society. As the Navajo story demonstrates, men and women must be together.

CONCLUSION

It is difficult in contemporary American society, and particularly in the highly structured environment of an academic institution, to comprehend the emotional and cognitive understanding of a landscape from which one can draw both physical and spiritual sustenance. It is, nevertheless, essential to a study of the bases for Native cultures to explore that relationship between human beings and their environments. Even though relatively few American Indians in contemporary society live on a daily basis in the intimate relationship with the land that their ancestors did, the memory of that relationship still persists as part of tribal identity. In some cases, as we will see in other chapters, the sense is one of loss. The stories of forced migrations under colonial powers or the US government create a particular historical circumstance. The political importance of land for tribal sovereignty is a unique dimension of Native identity in American society today. Native people are the ones who are indigenous to the land that is the United States today. Their relationship with it is unique as a source of cultural identity.

NOTES

1. Ronald Goodman, *Lakota Star Knowledge: Studies in Lakota Stellar Theology* (Rosebud, SD: Sinte Gleska University, 1992), p. 44.
2. James Mooney, *Myths of the Cherokee and Sacred Formulas of the Cherokees* (Nashville, TN: Charles and Randy Elder Booksellers, 1982), pp. 242–9.
3. Robert A. Warrior, 'A Native American perspective: Canaanites, cowboys, and Indians,' in *Voices from the Margin*, ed. R. S. Sugrtharajah (Maryknoll, NY: Orbis, 1995). Warrior compares the Hebrew invasion of the land of Canaan to the American colonization of Indian lands.
4. Vine Deloria, Jr, *God is Red: A Native View of Religion* (Golden, CO: North American Press, 1992), p. 67.
5. Elisabeth Tooker (ed.), *Native North American Spirituality of the Eastern Woodlands:*

Sacred Myths, Dreams, Visions, Speeches, Healing Formulas, Rituals, and Ceremonials
(New York: Paulist Press, 1979), pp. 36–7.

6. Stephen C. McCluskey, 'Historical archaeoastronomy: the Hopi example', from *Archaeoastronomy in the New World*, ed. by A. F. Aveni (Cambridge: Cambridge University Press, 1982), pp. 39–42.

7. Von Del Chamberlain, *When Stars Came Down to Earth: Cosmology of the Skidi Pawnee Indians of North America* (Los Altos, CA: Ballena; College Park, MD: Center for Archaeoastronomy, 1982); James R. Murie, *Ceremonies of the Pawnee*, ed. Douglas R. Parks (Lincoln: University of Nebraska Press, 1981), pp. 38–9.

8. John A. Eddy, 'Astronomical alignment of the Big Horn Medicine Wheel', *Science*, 1974, 184: 1,035–43.

9. Lynn Ceci, 'Watchers of the Pleiades: ethnoastronomy among Native cultivators in northeastern North America', *Ethnohistory*, 1978, 25: 301–17.

10. Ronald Goodman, *Lakota Star Knowledge*, pp. 3, 11.

11. Francis LaFlesche, 'The Osage tribe: two versions of the Child Naming Rite,' *Forty-Third Annual Report of the Bureau of American Ethnology (1925–26)* (Washington, DC: Government Printing Office, 1926), pp. 29–164.

12. Ibid., pp. 29–30.

13. Alice Lee Marriott and Carol K. Rachlin, *American Indian Mythology* (New York: Crowell, 1968), pp. 87–95.

14. Victor Barnouw, *Wisconsin Chippewa Myths and Tales and their Relation to Chippewa Life* (Madison: University of Wisconsin Press, 1977), pp. 14–40.

15. Goodman, *Lakota Star Knowledge*, pp. 44.

16. Benjamin Whorf, 'An American Indian model of the universe,' *Language, Thought, and Reality* (Cambridge, MA: Massachusetts Institute of Technology Press, 1970), pp. 59–60.

17. Hamilton A. Tyler, *Pueblo Gods and Myths* (Norman: University of Oklahoma Press, 1964), pp. 89–90.

18. Alfonso Ortiz, *The Tewa World; Space, Time, Being and Becoming in a Pueblo Society* (Chicago: University of Chicago Press, 1969), p. 98.

19. A. L. Kroeber, 'The World Renewal Cult of northwest California,' in *The California Indians: A Source Book*, 2nd edn, compiled and edited by R. F. Heizer and M. A. Whipple (Berkeley: University of California Press, 1971), pp. 464–71.

20. Gene Weltfish, *The Lost Universe* (New York: Basic Books, 1965), pp. 106–18.

21. Åke Hultkrantz, *Soul and Native Americans*, ed. Robert Holland (Woodstock, CT: Spring Publications, 1997), pp. 178–88; Hamilton A. Tyler, *Pueblo Gods and Myths* (Norman: University of Oklahoma Press, 1964), pp. 116–24.

22. Murray Wax, 'The notions of nature, man, and time of a hunting people,' *Southern Folklore Quarterly*, XXVI (Sept 1962), pp. 175–85.

23. Black Elk, *The Sacred Pipe: Black Elk's Account of the Seven Rites of the Oglala Sioux*, ed. Joseph Epes Brown (Norman: University of Oklahoma, 1953).

24. George Bird Grinnell, *The Fighting Cheyennes* (New York: C. Scribner's sons, 1915), p. 276.

25. Frank B. Linderman, *Plenty-Coups: Chief of the Crows* (New York: The John Day Company, 1930), pp. 61–7.

26. Don Talayesva, *Sun Chief: The Autobiography of a Hopi Indian*, ed. Leo W. Simmons (New Haven: Yale University Press, 1942), p. 45.
27. Don Talayesva, *Sun Chief*, pp. 81–4; Laura Thompson, 'Attitudes and acculturation,' *American Anthropologist*, n.s., L (1948), 200–15.
28. James Walker, *Lakota Belief and Ritual*, ed. by Raymond J. DeMallie and Elaine A. Jahner (Lincoln: University of Nebraska Press, 1980), p. 94.
29. Walker, *Lakota Belief and Ritual*; Basil Johnston. *The Manitous: The Spiritual World of the Ojibway* (New York: HarperCollins, 1995); J. N. B. Hewitt, 'Orenda and a Definition of Religion,' *American Anthropologist*, n.s., IV (1902), 33–46.
30. Paul Radin, *The Trickster; A Study in American Indian Mythology* (New York: Schocken Books, 1956), xi–xxii; Jace Weaver, *Other Words: American Indian Literature, Law and Culture* (Norman: University of Oklahoma Press, 2001), pp. 246–57.
31. Victor Barnouw, *Wisconsin Chippewa Myths and Tales*, pp. 14–40.
32. Berard Haile, *Navajo Coyote Tales: The Curly Tó Aheedlíinii Version*, ed. Karl W. Luckert (Lincoln: University of Nebraska Press, 1984), pp. 7–8.
33. Alice Lee Marriott, *Saynday's People: The Kiowa Indians and the Stories They Told* (Lincoln: University of Nebraska Press, 1947), pp. 3–12.
34. Ibid., pp. 44–52, 75–7.
35. Paul Radin, *The Trickster*, pp. 26–7.
36. Richard Erdoes and Alfonso Ortiz (eds), *American Indian Myths and Legends* (New York: Pantheon Books, 1984), pp. 379–80.
37. Mircea Eliade, *Shamanism; Archaic Techniques of Ecstasy* (Princeton: Princeton University Press, 1964), p. 32.
38. Talayesva, *Sun Chief*, pp. 190–1.
39. Barbara Tedlock, *The Beautiful and the Dangerous: Encounters with the Zuni Indians* (New York: Viking, 1992); Louis A. Hieb, 'Meaning and mismeaning: toward an understanding of the Ritual Clown', *New Perspectives on the Pueblos*, ed. Alfonso Ortiz (Albuquerque: University of New Mexico Press, 1972), pp. 170–4.
40. *Black Elk Speaks: Being the Life Story of a Holy Man of the Oglala Sioux*, as told to John G. Neihardt (Lincoln: University of Nebraska Press, 1961).
41. Keith H. Basso, *Wisdom Sits in Places: Landscape and Language Among the Western Apache* (Albuquerque: University of New Mexico Press, 1996), pp. 25–7.
42. Berard Haile, *Women Versus Men; A Conflict of Navajo Emergence* (Lincoln: University of Nebraska Press, 1981), pp. 13–35.
43. John C. Ewers, *Plains Indian History and Culture: Essays on Continuity and Change* (Norman: University of Oklahoma, 1997).
44. John G. Neihardt, *When the Tree Flowered; An Authentic Tale of the Old Sioux World* (New York: Macmillan, 1951).

CHAPTER 3

Historical Contact and Conflict

Our second premise is that the cultural contact between Indians and Europeans must be seen from the perspectives of both sides. We propose not a complete counter-narrative from a strictly Native point of view, but rather a recognition of the fact that Indian people have their own accounts of these intercultural encounters, which may differ significantly from those of Europeans, and which play an essential role in understanding how they viewed their role.

Key to the premise is the understanding that there are distinctive aspects of Indian views of history. Oral narratives and place names constitute parts of this uniquely Native perspective on the past. As we have pointed out, Indians regard cycles of events – that is, repetition – as more important than a linear narrative of unique events and change, which constitutes our contemporary academic notion of history. Indians were and are, however, able to deal with the unique events in their own way. Plains Indians' winter counts, images painted in spiral fashion on hides, record a significant event for each year.[1] Communities may preserve the memory of events in stories and ceremonies. Alfonso Ortiz, a Tewa from San Juan Pueblo and professor of anthropology at the University of New Mexico, described how Jesse Jackson, presidential candidate in 1984, went to the Hopi reservation to campaign for votes. He gave a speech in his distinctive, often rhyming, rhetoric. In the next major ceremonial in that community, a clown appeared dressed in a pinstriped suit and an orange Afro-style wig and proceeded to deliver a reprise of Jackson's speech in the Hopi language. As Ortiz explained, the clown represented the Hopi way of integrating a unique event into their own sense of history.[2] If he continued to appear in future ceremonies, then Jesse Jackson would be part of Hopi history. If not, the Hopi would have dismissed Jackson as irrelevant. In Ortiz's story particularly, we find one of the distinctions between local knowledge and global knowledge that is essential to Native American Studies. What is important to Native communities is how the unique event may affect their own lives, not the global understanding of history.

Local histories and global histories represent two ways of understanding events that change the patterns of human life. The premise of this chapter is concerned with intercultural contact situations as historical phenomena because they are the beginning of significant changes for both Natives and Europeans, and in that sense they are important to the academic enterprise in which we are engaged. Inherent in our premise is the assumption that Indians are active agents in their history, not simply passive victims or obstacles to someone else's progress.

The narrative of American history that dominates public education in the United States still generally portrays Indians as the helpless victims of a militarily and culturally superior civilization. In the 1970s, both popular books, such as Dee Brown's *Bury My Heart at Wounded Knee* and Ralph Andrist's *The Long Death*, and the scholarly book *The Conquest of America*, by Francis Jennings, emphasized the atrocities perpetrated against Indians.[3] It was not until James Merrell demonstrated how the Catawba in South Carolina survived as a tribe that Indian agency became recognized as a major factor in history. The Catawba maintained a covert sense of identity through kinship ties even as they lost their lands and largely ceased to be recognized as Indians by surrounding black and white populations.[4]

It is relatively recently that historians have begun to acknowledge the roles of Indians as agents in history. There is a new emphasis on including the voices of people who have not been heard before. The fact that American Indians did not have written languages has meant that their viewpoints had long been excluded from the academic study of history, which principally depends upon written records. Indian voices in the early historical record must be reconstructed from European accounts. European missionaries, among the most literate of early colonizers, were also often astute ethnographers who recorded voluminous details of the cultures of those they wished to convert to Christianity; however, their culturally-based assumptions about Native people strongly colored their judgments.

The joining of aspects of anthropology with history produced the field of ethnohistory in the 1950s. The method known as 'upstreaming' involves determining cultural practices in contemporary communities and studying historical accounts of those communities to search for persistent practices, attitudes, and explanations that indicate continuity.[5] Although the ethno-historical method has come under criticism for over-insistence on elements of cultural continuity, many scholars understand its usefulness as an inter-pretive tool to understand the cultural dimensions of historical knowledge. The most important thing about ethnohistory as a method is its insistence on attention to cultural perspective, and its recognition of the fact that cul-tures are dynamic rather than static.[6]

The establishment of ethnohistory in the academy has resulted in the inclusion of Native voices in the writing of history, challenging the osten-sibly objective examination of the human past in the academy. Objectivity presupposes a neutral stance and an omniscient third-party observer of events, but, as scholars like historian Hayden White and anthropologist James Clifford have argued, pure academic objectivity is an impossibility.[7]

Another factor that complicates the study of the history of intercultural contact is that many oral narratives of historical episodes have been filed under the academic category of folklore, which says something in itself about how Native versions of historical events have been viewed by non-Indian scholars. However, such narratives can prove to be valuable accounts of events of the distant past. William Simmons's study of Passamoquody and Narragansett narratives demonstrates the value of such allusions, for instance, in accounts of early encounters with black people and the building of the first bridge from an island community to the mainland.[8]

Indian ways of telling their past are essentially different from European ways of writing history; Indian voices must be heard, and their understand-ing of their interactions with Europeans must be part of historical accounts. The inclusion of these perspectives has led to new interpretations in the writing of American history by both Native and non-Native scholars. Indian historians have introduced tribal perspectives into the histories of their own tribes,[9] and non-Indian historians have increasingly paid atten-tion to cultural identity in the process of historical change.[10]

The result of the inclusion of Native voices is not only to prove that Indians were active participants in their encounters with European colo-nists, but to show how both Native and non-Native cultures changed as a result of their contacts.[11] Richard White's *The Middle Ground* describes attempts of Indians and European colonists to negotiate common under-standings from cultural differences.[12] The result was not a totally homoge-neous new culture but the establishment of new communities where

Natives and colonists could achieve a greater understanding of each other. Although the concept of a 'middle ground' as White explicates it was a historical phenomenon in that it happened in a particular area at a particular time in American history, it has become commonly used to study intercultural contact with attention to cultural understandings on the part of both groups involved.

Native people supplied the English colonists at Plymouth and Jamestown with the food that allowed them to survive their first winter in their new homes. The first Thanksgiving, idealized in American history, was not a gathering of equals but the colonists' acknowledgement of their dependence on the Indians. Indians were shrewd negotiators diplomatically. They were also shrewd traders, and they were quite capable of playing both ends against the middle in the wars that went on throughout the period between colonial powers.

As some of the cherished myths of American history have been discredited – George Washington did not, indeed, chop down the cherry tree and confess the deed to his father – history told from tribal perspectives has led to new understanding of some questionable historical traditions. Pocahontas did not save John Smith out of love, but in order to adopt him as a kinsman to establish a relationship that would allow the colonists and the Powhatans to live together in peace.[13] Although the Walt Disney movie *Pocahontas* perpetuates the myth of romantic love between the beautiful Indian maiden and the handsome white man, from the cultural perspective of a Powhatan woman, John Smith became a relative, and when Pocahontas met John Smith in England after she had married John Rolfe, she reaffirmed that kinship relationship.[14]

Early diplomatic relationships between Europeans and Indians reveal diverse perspectives based on different notions of kinship. French rhetoric cast the Indians as children who must be subservient to their French 'fathers.' The Indians, in turn, dutifully responded with speeches that expressed their dependency on the French. What the Frenchmen did not realize was that in the kinship systems of the Indians, the father was a relatively powerless figure. Rather, the maternal uncle was the person who had the greatest responsibility for the well-being of his sister's children. The rhetoric of the French defeated their purposes, while Indians used their own rhetoric of dependency as a tool with which they could acquire trade goods.[15] The anthropological idea of fictive kinship relationships is useful for understanding how Indian ideas about familial obligations were mechanisms for establishing relationships with European colonists.

In the American southwest, Indian communities constantly encountered explorers and missionaries who had little respect for their beliefs. Father Benavides, a Spanish Franciscan priest, disparaged the Navajo faith of native healers, urging them instead to touch the cross that he carried in order to be healed by the Christian God.[16] In northeastern North America, Jesuit missionaries sought to force the Indians into a state of Christian submissiveness to the will of God. In Catholic theology, the Indians were guilty of the sin of pride, the idea that they were the equals of God. In their own beliefs, however, the Indians were able to establish personal relationships with spiritual forces through dreams and visions. Those relationships allowed men to influence the actions of the spiritual world. What to the Jesuits was the sin of pride was the very essence of native beliefs.[17]

European trade goods, such as copper kettles, guns, traps and cloth, changed Indian lifestyles irrevocably. They brought about major changes in the ways in which Indians hunted and clothed themselves, but they did not substantially alter their world views. The new goods were adopted as analogous to traditional items. Trade beads were similar to naturally occurring crystals used for divination. Guns replicated thunder, a powerful natural force. Copper kettles were used for cooking, but they were also buried with the dead, as was native pottery.[18]

Although warfare was a factor in population decline in Native communities, scholarly attention in the 1970s and after focused increasingly on the role that European-introduced diseases played in that decline.[19] Indeed, historical demography became an important, and sometimes contentious field as scholars attempted to come to some definitive figure for aboriginal populations as a baseline for decline.[20] Depopulation was generally interpreted by Europeans as God's act, as John Winthrop phrased it, 'to clear the land for the Sons of Adam,' while Indians often interpreted it as punishment for their acceptance of European customs and goods. Even the decline of animal populations was interpreted as the animals' withdrawal from human contact because of the new ways of hunting.[21]

The impact of disease was not merely the loss of population but the disruption of the highly structured social relationships of obligation and reciprocity that held Native communities together. That destruction and the overwhelming flood of English settlers on the eastern seaboard soon began to overwhelm Indian communities. Indian resistance to white settlement became increasingly violent. In the south, Opechancanough, the nephew of Powhatan, led a major attack on settlements around Jamestown in 1622. In New England, Metacom, known to the English as King Phillip, led his followers in attacks on frontier villages in 1675, thus introducing the indelible image of the hostile savage into the American consciousness.[22]

Warfare was not simply a response to the threat that Europeans posed to Native communities. It was spiritually sanctioned. The Ottawa leader Pontiac acted under the guidance of the Delaware prophet Neolin. The Shawnee Tecumseh attempted to build an Indian coalition to drive the Europeans out of the United States based on his brother Tenskwatawa's spiritual visions.[23]

The failure of Pontiac and Tecumseh to achieve their ends of concerted action against the whites was as much a result of the persistence of tribal identities as of American military superiority. Indians saw no racial basis to provide a sense of common purpose against European settlement. The impact of war and trade brought Indians and Europeans into contact on an intimate basis and required new ways of cross-cultural communication. Intermarriage between European men and Indian women became an important factor in cross-cultural communication, and the children of these unions created new kinds of communities. The relationship between early colonial governments and the US government and the Indian tribes was defined by treaties based on the status of tribes as sovereign nations. Early treaties simply established peace and friendship between tribes and colonial governments and the United States. As Indian tribes lost population to disease, as their hunting grounds were depleted of game, and as they were defeated in battle, the treaties that they signed increasingly led to agreements to place themselves under the protection of the US government and to cede much of their lands. These treaties did not interfere with the tribes' exercise of their own self-governance; they did, however, introduce the problem of jurisdiction of Indian tribes over non-Indians within their lands, and as European population grew, colonial governments were increasingly unable to police the actions of their citizens on the frontier.

As the United States emerged as the dominant political power in North America after the Revolutionary War, the conduct of relations with the Indians became the government's major preoccupation, not only because trade with Indian nations was still a viable economic enterprise, but because it needed Indian land. Soldiers in the Revolutionary army were paid in land scrip, paper certificates that they could use to claim and settle on public lands, but the government had first to clear Indians from the land. The sale of public land, that is, Indian land acquired by treaty, was the major source of revenue for the government which was still deeply in debt in the first years after the Revolution.

Americans were often unscrupulous in their dealings with Indians. President Thomas Jefferson saw Indian trading debts as an incentive for Indians to cede land to pay those debts, while he himself was a land speculator.[24] Chief Justice John Marshall formulated the legal argument in 1824 that Indians did not have title to their lands in the Western sense but enjoyed only the right of occupancy. Although he acknowledged the rights of tribes to govern their own internal affairs in two important decisions in 1831 and 1832, he defined the relationship of tribes to the federal government as that of 'dependent domestic nations.'[25] Marshall's decisions were followed by Indian removal, the federal policy of removing Indians from lands east of the Mississippi River to the western territory acquired by the United States in the Louisiana Purchase.

The issue of removal caused deep divisions in tribes, and it inspired diverse and strongly opposing opinions among Christian missionary leaders, government bureaucrats, and common people hungry for new lands to settle. There were reasoned opinions both for and against removal in both Indian and white communities. The rhetoric of removal as federal policy was that the uncivilized Indians must be removed from the pernicious influences of white frontier society before they were overrun and totally destroyed by it. Read another way, the rhetoric revealed the political reality that white men wanted Indian land. Studies of the removal policy and its effects have contributed to our understanding of the forces of historical change that were at work within Indian communities as well as of the changes in the relationship between tribes and the US government.[26]

The act confronted southeastern tribes with the political reality that peaceful coexistence with white populations was impossible. A significant part of the Cherokee population in Georgia was civilized, to all intents and purposes. They had schools and churches, a written language in the Cherokee syllabary, a newspaper, *The Cherokee Phoenix*, published in English and Cherokee, a written constitution and laws.[27] The neighboring Choctaws, Chickasaws, and Creeks had adopted many practices from their white neighbors. But as the states of Georgia, Alabama, and Mississippi extended their laws and jurisdiction over the Cherokees, Creeks, Choctaws, and Chickasaws within their boundaries, the tribes were faced with the dilemma of staying in their homelands (the primary source of their cultural identity) or maintaining their tribal identity as self-governing nations by moving west of the Mississippi River. The fact is that the removal period was not a simple black (or red) and white case of a conflict between hostile savages and civilized American society. It was a highly complex interaction of motives both selfish and altruistic, cultural and political, idealistic and mundane. Historical analysis of those motives enriches our understanding that both American society and tribal cultures were changing rapidly, and in some ways that understanding makes even more poignant and tragic the ultimate removal of Indian tribes to the west.

Given Georgia's insistence that the US government fulfill a promise to remove Indians from its boundaries, and given Andrew Jackson's determination to rid the United States of tribes as sovereign enclaves within the United States, it was clear that Indian nations had virtually no choice in the matter. Removal treaties were signed by small factions of tribes and, in the case of the Cherokees and Creeks, promptly repudiated by other leaders. Although some of the Cherokees moved west voluntarily, for the rest the forced removal of 1838 became known as the Trail of Tears, or Nunna daul Tsunyi.

The general perception that all Indians left the southeast during the removal period is inaccurate: recent studies demonstrate that Indians did not entirely disappear from the region, and that loss of homeland did not negate their sense of identity. Instead, groups who escaped removal used various strategies to maintain communities. Although many of these studies have been undertaken by anthropologists rather than historians, they collect the voices of people who often express their own sense of the historical persistence of the tribal identity.[28]

The tribes of the northeast and the Ohio River Valley were dispossessed of their lands early in the nineteenth century as a result of war. Their cessions of land were largely forced, and they began a trek that would eventually lead them to settlement in what is now the state of Oklahoma.[29] The tribes of the Plains, who were to encounter the press of American expansionism in the era of Manifest Destiny, and whose sense of homeland was much different from that of the southeastern tribes, ceded lands they had always used for hunting. At stake for these tribes was freedom to move without restriction over the territories that they had traditionally used, a freedom finally constrained by treaties that confined them to reservations and maintained them there in part through military force.[30]

The ultimate fate of most Indian tribes in the late nineteenth century was really a foregone conclusion based on federal policy to divide Indian land into individual plots that individuals would hold as private property and to subsume Indian Territory into the United States. The idea was not new in the late nineteenth century. Indeed, its roots were deeply embedded in the Jeffersonian ideal of the yeoman farmer, and its intent became clear in the debate over the Kansas-Nebraska bill in 1854. It was implicit in the expansion of railroads and the desire to drive them through Indian Territory. It was subsumed in the debate over slavery, that is, free soil or slave territory, which was in turn complicated by the fact that one aspect of civilization adopted by the Cherokee, Choctaws, Chickasaws, and Creeks was the institution of slavery.[31]

The Five Tribes (now including the Seminoles) fought with the Confederacy, although again, their participation in the war was the cause of deep tribal divisions. After the war, the United States argued treason, while the tribes argued that the United States had abrogated its treaty obligation to protect the tribes by withdrawing its forces from Indian Territory in the face of Confederate advances. A plan for allotment of land and extension of a federal Territorial government was written into the treaties that the tribes were forced to sign after the war. It was clear that the United States planned to 'reconstruct' the tribes as part of a state within the United States.

If the rhetoric of the early nineteenth century was to save the Indians from extinction by removing them from contact with white society, the rhetoric of the latter part of the century was to give them the civilizing benefits of their own homes, private property, and American citizenship, and to assimilate them into American society.[32] Ironically, the Act came at a time when the life of the yeoman farmer was far from ideal, as evidenced by the rise of the Populist Party, the existence of the Granger Movement, and the struggle over currency reform to relieve farmers from crushing debts. That the Dawes Act proposed an agrarian model that was proving dysfunctional in the face of an increasingly industrialized society speaks as much to its hope for American social and political reform and the destruction of both land and corporate monopolies as it does to its naivety about Indians.

The policy of allotment was embodied in the General Allotment Act of 1887 (also known as the Dawes Act after its sponsor, Senator Henry L. Dawes of Massachusetts). The Five Tribes and several others in the Indian Territory were exempt from the act, the Five Tribes because they held fee simple title to their lands from the Federal government. But the Indian Territory now was home to a rapidly growing population of white entrepreneurs and laborers hired by Indians who lived without any form of government or protection of laws. In order to extend federal law over the white population and give them rights to claim land upon which they already lived, Congress appointed a commission headed by Henry Dawes to convince the Five Tribes to accept allotment, and their coerced agreement to do so was embodied in the Curtis Act, passed in 1898.

Allotment destroyed the land base of many tribes as individual owners sold or were cheated out of their land. It challenged the identity of American Indians as a people associated with the land. Its long-term effects undermined Indian senses of communal identity as people sold or lost land and moved away to urban areas, although in the short term it may have reinforced them in a negative way since individuals who had land took in their kin who had lost their lands under the allotment process.[33]

The other major agent of cultural assimilation of American Indians in the late nineteenth and early twentieth centuries was the boarding school. Although boarding schools have been generally portrayed as destructive to American Indian cultures (and certainly their stated purposes were, as Richard Henry Pratt, founder of Carlisle Indian School in Pennsylvania (1879) declared, to kill the Indian in order to preserve the man), recent scholarship on boarding schools from the perspectives of the students therein reveals that they served an important role as vehicles for cultural preservation, in the form of resistance to non-Indian authority. As Tsianina Lomawaima points out in her study of Chilocco Boarding School in Oklahoma, students formed friendships that lasted beyond the school years, friendships that reinforced a sense of Indian identity. They also found inventive ways to subvert the authority that schools tried to impose upon them. Brenda Child points out in her study of boarding schools where Chippewa students were sent that schools sometimes provided a nurturing environment for students whose own home lives had been totally disrupted by poverty and often the death of a parent. Clyde Ellis's study of the Rainy Mountain Boarding School in Oklahoma, which served primarily Kiowa children, shows that the school did not totally destroy the Indian identity of its students, and that the school's staff suffered as much from financial neglect by the federal government as did the students.[34] The contribution to scholarship in the field of history of education has been a much more nuanced view of the boarding school experience.

Fred Hoxie has argued persuasively that the perceived failure of Indians to assimilate into American society led to the disillusionment of liberal reformers and a return to a general notion of the wardship status of American Indians.[35] The shift in federal policy away from assimilation came gradually in the early twentieth century. The impoverishment of Indians because of the effects of allotment, and the often overcrowded and unhealthy conditions in boarding schools were brought to light in the Meriam report of 1928. The report, undertaken by the Institute for Government Affairs (the forerunner of the present day Brookings Institute) under the direction of Louis Meriam, revealed unsanitary water supplies, inadequate housing, widespread incidence of disease (including high rates of tuberculosis and trachoma in the boarding schools), and general incompetence in the administration of services for Indians by the Bureau of Indian Affairs. However, the report blamed most of the problems of Indian poverty on the fact that Indians leased their land to non-Indians and lived off 'unearned income' rather than applying themselves to farming. Its main solution to the problems of Indian administration was to increase the education budget so Indians could learn how to live the lives of good American citizens.[36]

The onset of the Great Depression in 1929 ended any hope of major funding for Indian-related initiatives, but it did pave the way for Franklin Roosevelt's New Deal. The policies of John Collier, Roosevelt's Commissioner of Indian Affairs, began a movement in the direction of restoration of tribal sovereignty. Collier believed in supporting the communal cultures of the tribes, cultures badly damaged by the Dawes Act. He said, 'Clan instinct, clan operation of assets, is inherent in [Indians]. The tribal Indian remains the self-reliant and self-supporting Indian.'[37] The Wheeler-Howard (or Indian Reorganization) Act, passed in 1934, put into effect Collier's policies on self-government, preservation of religion and culture, economic opportunity, and communal land ownership, even though Congress watered down his original proposals. After years of steady decline, Indian economic fortunes finally began to rebound.

The Indian Reorganization Act (IRA) was, at the time of its passage, a highly controversial piece of legislation, both in Congress and among members of Indian tribes. Although Collier has been portrayed as a visionary reformer, and indeed his own writings reflect a highly romanticized notion of the integrity of Indian cultures, his policies were not widely accepted by American Indians. Because Collier respected the rights of Indians to govern themselves, tribes had to vote whether to accept the terms of the act, and a number opted not to do so. The Act remains controversial today. With its emphasis on economic development and self sufficiency, it is also read by Vine Deloria, Jr and Clifford Lytle as an early form of the termination policy that would later be implemented by the Federal government in the 1950s. What the IRA did accomplish, as Deloria and Lytle argue, was to establish a principle of the inherent sovereignty of tribes, and that principle came not in the act itself but in an opinion by Attorney General Nathan Margold asserting that tribal sovereignty was inherent rather than delegated by Congress.[38]

The Second World War drew 25,000 Indians into the Armed Forces, and many to employment in war plants. Many veterans returned from the war with an expanded view of American society and its opportunities, although many had also experienced overt racism in the Armed Services.[39] During the war, the government had significantly reduced the size of the Bureau of Indian Affairs and moved it out of Washington to Chicago. After the war, the federal government's attempt to downsize itself, and the general prosperity of American society in the post-war economic boom, led to the formation of policy to terminate the federal responsibility to American Indians, embodied by Congress in House Resolution 108, passed in 1953. Dillon Myer, the man who oversaw the internment of the Japanese during the Second World War, became Commissioner of Indian Affairs and began the program of removing tribes from their special relationship with the federal government, thereby eliminating federal services. An aspect of the termination policy was the relocation of Indians from reservations to major urban areas where, it was assumed, they would find ready employment because of the thriving US economy.[40] Although Indians had been migrating to cities for years, the relocation policy of the early 1950s created new communities, pan-tribal in their make-up but still a significant source of Indian identity. Although life in urban American often exposed Indians to racism and hostility, and its economic benefits were often far overrated (themes developed in the burgeoning field of Native American literature), scholars have begun to explore the strength of those communities as sources of individual and group identity.[41]

If the goal of termination was to make Indians more self-sufficient by taking away federal funds and thus to save government money, it failed miserably. In terminating the Menominee in Wisconsin, for instance, the federal government spent $5 million in special aid, the state of Wisconsin spent $1 million in additional funds, while healthcare, education, and the Menominee economy were greatly weakened. In the case of virtually every tribe, termination weakened self-sufficiency, reduced vital services, and ended up costing the government more money than it otherwise would have spent.[42]

Relocation and termination were no more effective solutions to problems of poverty and poor health among Indian people than removal and allotment had been, but urban Indian centers in the 1960s became places where Indian voices began to speak out very audibly against racism and oppression. The takeover of Alcatraz Island in San Francisco Bay in November 1969 was organized by a Chippewa businessman living San Francisco, and the first wave of occupiers was composed largely of college students from Bay Area institutions. The event attracted major media attention across the nation, although it ended with a whimper when the last few occupiers were removed by the Coast Guard in the spring of 1971.[43] The American Indian Movement emerged out of police harassment of Indians in the Franklin Avenue neighborhood of Minneapolis, and achieved its media prominence with the takeover in 1972 of a store in the village of Wounded Knee, South Dakota, site of a massacre of some 300 Lakota people in 1890.[44] The other major wellspring of Indian activism – protests over restrictions on Indian fishing rights on the northwest coast – also gained attention when actor Marlon Brando espoused the Indians' cause.[45] The rise of the Red Power movement has been a fertile field for research because it has allowed scholars to present Indian perspectives on both their history and their conditions in the mid-twentieth century.

CONCLUSION

The challenge of telling history from a native perspective in the later part of the nineteenth century is that the cultures of tribes had been so disrupted by depopulation, Christian missionary efforts, and loss of their land base that much of their knowledge of the past has been lost. Culture is, however, a dynamic process. In a historical sense, it is always changing and adapting to new circumstances. And this is one of the challenges that Native American Studies faces in dealing with cultural contact: to demonstrate a sense of Indian identity while recognizing the cultural adaptation that tribes have undergone over time.

The writing of American Indian history has also introduced new methodologies. The academic discipline of history is a construction of a particular time and place (the ancient Greek world) that has evolved within the subsequent Western intellectual tradition of skepticism and objectivity. Native history is also a construction of time and place, but with much difference meanings, that is, cyclical time and the spirituality of place.

Indian intellectuals have seen history as a European colonial enterprise devoted to undermining the integrity of Indian cultures and communities, and Native American Studies scholars have called for a new relationship between historians and Native people in which respect and reciprocity prevail. Historians, they insist, must let Indian communities determine what they need in the way of knowledge to protect their rights and interests.

Communities must have the final authority over the texts that historians produce because community members are the ultimate source of knowledge of their own histories. This stance seems to fly in the face of historical objectivity in the academic sense, but it is a powerful statement about the ultimate subjectivity of historical knowledge.[46]

The field of Native American Studies has moved Indians out of the role of passive victims in an inevitable historical process and into the role of active participants in a process of change and adaptation that has affected both parties in intercultural encounters. It challenges a still widely prevalent belief in the US that all the 'real Indians' died off by 1890, overwhelmed by American military superiority and their inability to adapt to new ways of life. Native American Studies balances the tensions between federal policies and societal forces pushing Indians to assimilate completely into American society and Native strategies of adapting aspects of Anglo society as a means of survival for their communities.

By looking for Indian voices in cultural encounters and hearing them from a cultural viewpoint, Native American Studies can examine the expectations held by parties in the encounter, and how they were fulfilled (if, indeed, they were fulfilled) at some historical moment. Studies of missionary efforts among American Indian tribes can reveal the irony of the historical doctrine of unintended consequences. Missionaries wanted to convert Indians to Christianity, but Indians wanted schools so they could learn to better cope with white society. The federal government saw Christianity as a means to accomplish a policy of assimilating Indians into American society, whereas Indian communities often subverted churches into centers for community activities that reinforced markers of identity such as language (preaching and hymns in Native languages), community feasts, and stickball games in the southeast.[47] The number of books on Native American history has grown tremendously since the 1970s, and they document the persistence of Native communities by demonstrating that cultural change does not mean total assimilation.[48]

If the writing of history by non-Natives has been a colonialist act that has imposed the colonizer's meaning on the Native American past, then contemporary scholars have adopted the academy's term in calling for the de-colonizing of Native American Studies. A part of that call is for the establishment of a code of professional ethics in the field. What are the responsibilities of researchers to the communities whose history they study?

In the Western tradition, history is generally composed of accounts of the actions of individuals. In contemporary America, however, Native scholars hold up the sense of community as one of the markers of Indian identity.[49] In casual conversation, 'the community' is held up as the touch-stone for cultural authority. The term implies a sense of respect for and deference to a collective sense of cultural values and appropriate behavior, and a sense of responsibility to the group. In this sense, the scholar who enters the community becomes, then, not the expert but truly a student learning from the elders who express the shared memory of the community. It also means, however, that the scholar must put aside the skepticism concerning sources that the academic world expects in its search for objectivity, and must become, in effect, the voice of 'the community.'

Should scholars be responsible to communities by their histories as they hear them from the elders? Here again we confront the challenge of local knowledge and global knowledge. Native histories are found in oral traditions, what is often labeled as folklore. It often does not match written sources. It is very much the story of day-to-day life in communities. If one of the goals of Native American Studies programs is to educate non-Indians about Indians, then we come back to the epistemological question, how can non-Natives understand a truly Native narrative as 'history' in the academic sense?

The problem is illustrated by such books as Patricia Nelson Limerick's *Legacy of Conquest* and Richard White's *Its Your Misfortune and None of my Own*, part of the canon of the New Western History.[50] Both have been controversial among professional historians with their insistence that the stories of all groups involved in the formation of Western society be represented. By challenging an established narrative of American progress and the triumph of modern industrial society, these books have de-centered American history.

The challenge to Native American/American Indian Studies, then, is to bring to the fore the perspectives of Native people, to establish the legitimacy of their way of telling their own histories, and because they have been a part of American history in their interactions with European colonists, to assure that their motives and actions are fully represented.

NOTES

1. Russell Thornton, 'A Rosebud Reservation winter count, circa 1751–1752 to 1886–1887,' *Ethnohistory* 49: 4 (Fall 2002), 725–41.
2. Alfonso Ortiz, presentation at National Endowment for the Humanities Summer Institute for College Teachers, 'Myth, memory and history, new approaches to

writing American Indian History,' The Newberry Library, Chicago, Illinois, June
1990.

3. Dee Brown, *Bury My Heart at Wounded Knee: An Indian History of the American
    West* (New York: Holt, Rinehart and Winston, 1970); Ralph K. Andrist, *The Long
    Death: the Last Days of the Plains Indian* (Norman: University of Oklahoma Press,
    2001); Francis Jennings, *The Invasion of America* (Chapel Hill: University of North
    Carolina Press, 1975).

4. James H. Merrell, *The Indians' New World: Catawbas and their Neighbors from
    European Contact through the Era of Removal* (Chapel Hill: published for the Institute
    of Early American History and Culture, Williamsburg, VA by the University of
    North Carolina Press, 1989).

5. William N. Fenton, 'Ethnohistory and its problems,' *Ethnohistory*, 9, no. 1 (Winter
    1962), 12. Fenton first used the technique in his article, 'Iroquois suicide: a study in
    the stability of a culture pattern,' *Bureau of American Ethnology Bulletin 128*
    (Washington: Government Printing Office, 1941), pp. 79–137.

6. For a current critique of ethnohistory, see Melissa Meyer and Kerwin Klein, 'Native
    American Studies and the end of ethnohistory,' in Russell Thornton (ed.), *Studying
    Native America: Problems and Prospects* (Madison: University of Wisconsin Press,
    1998).

7. Peter Novick, *That Noble Dream: the 'Objectivity Question' and the American
    Historical Profession* (Cambridge: Cambridge University Press, 1988); Hayden V.
    White, *Tropics of Discourse: Essays in Cultural Criticism* (Baltimore: Johns Hopkins
    Press, 1978); James Clifford, *The Predicament of Culture: Twentieth-century
    Ethnography, Literature and Art* (Cambridge, MA: Harvard University Press,
    1988).

8. William S. Simmons, *Spirit of the New England Tribes: Indian History and Folklore
    1620–1984* (Hanover: University Press of New England, 1986).

9. John Joseph Mathews, *The Osages, Children of the Middle Waters* (Norman:
    University of Oklahoma Press, 1961); Joe Sando, *Nee Hemish, a History of Jemez
    Pueblo* (Albuquerque: University of New Mexico Press, 1982); Alan Slickpoo, *Noon
    nee-me-poo (We, the Nez Perces). Culture and History of the Nez Perces* (Lapwai, ID:
    Nez Perce Tribe of Idaho, 1973–); Steven J. Crum, *The Road on Which We Came =
    Po'i pentun tammen kimmappeh: a History of the Western Shoshone* (Salt Lake City:
    University of Utah Press, 1994).

10. James H. Merrell, *The Indians' New World: Catawbas and their Neighbors from
    European Contact through the Era of Removal* (Chapel Hill: published for the Institute
    of Early American History and Culture, Williamsburg, VA, by the University of
    North Carolina Press, 1989); Daniel Richter, *Facing East from Indian Country: a
    Native History of Early America* (Cambridge, MA: Harvard University Press, 2001);
    Daniel K. Richter, *The Ordeal of the Longhouse: the Peoples of the Iroquois League in
    the Era of European Colonization* (Chapel Hill: published for the Institute of Early
    American History and Culture, Williamsburg, VA by the University of North
    Carolina Press, 1992).

11. Colin G. Calloway, *New Worlds for All: Indians, Europeans, and the Remaking of Early
    America* (Baltimore: Johns Hopkins University Press, 1997).

12. Richard White, *The Middle Ground: Indians, Empires, and Republics in the Great Lakes Region, 1650–1815* (Cambridge and New York: Cambridge University Press, 1991).

13. Frederic Gleach, *Powhatan's World and Colonial Virginia: a Conflict of Cultures* (Lincoln: University of Nebraska Press, 1997); Clara Sue Kidwell, 'Indian women as cultural mediators,' *Ethnohistory* 39: 2 (Spring 1992), 97–107.

14. Capt. John Smith, *Works, 1608–1631*, ed. Edward Arber (Birmingham, UK, 1884), pp. 498–9.

15. Patricia Galloway, 'The Chief who is your father: Choctaw and French views of the diplomatic relation,' in Peter H. Wood, Gregory A. Waselkov, and M. Thomas Hatley *Powhatan's Mantle: Indians in the Colonial Southeast* (Lincoln: University of Nebraska Press, 1989), pp. 254–78.

16. Fray Alonso de Benavides, *Alonso de Benavides' Revised Memorial of 1634; with Numerous Supplementary Documents Elaborately Annotated*, ed. and trans. by Frederick Webb Hodge, George P. Hammond and Agapito Rey (Coronado cuarto centennial publications, 1540–1940; vol. IV, Albuquerque: The University of New Mexico Press, 1945).

17. James Axtell, *The Invasion Within: the Contest of Cultures in Colonial North America* (New York: Oxford University Press, 1985).

18. Calvin Martin, 'The four lives of a Micmac copper pot,' *Ethnohistory* 22: 2 (Spring 1975), 111–33; Laurier Turgeon, 'The tale of the kettle: odyssey of an intercultural object,' *Ethnohistory* 44:1 (Winter 1997), 1–29; Christopher J. Miller and George R. Hamell, 'A new perspective on Indian-white contact: cultural symbols and colonial trade,' *Journal of American History*, 73, no. 2 (September 1986), 311–28.

19. Henry F. Dobyns, *Their Number Become Thinned: Native American Population Dynamics in Eastern North America* (Knoxville: University of Tennessee Press, 1983); Ann Ramanofsky, *Vectors of Death* (Albuquerque: University of New Mexico Press, 1987); Russell Thornton, *American Indian Holocaust and Survival: a Population History since 1492* (Norman: University of Oklahoma Press, 1987).

20. David P. Henige, *Numbers from Nowhere: The American Indian Contact Population Debate* (Norman: University of Oklahoma Press, 1998.

21. Calvin Martin, *Keepers of the Game: Indian-animal Relationships and the Fur Trade* (Berkeley: University of California Press, 1978). Martin's interpretation was criticized by anthropologists for being overly broad. See, for example, Adrian Tanner, *Bringing Home Animals: Religious Ideology and Mode of Production of the Mistassini Cree Hunters* (New York: St. Martin's Press, 1979).

22. Jill Lepore, *The Name of War: King Philip's War and the Origins of American Identity* (New York: Knopf, 1998).

23. Gregory Evans Dowd, *A Spirited Resistance: the North American Indian Struggle for Unity, 1745–1815* (Baltimore: Johns Hopkins University Press, 1992); R. David Edmunds, *The Shawnee Prophet* (Lincoln: University of Nebraska Press, 1983); Joel W. Martin, *Sacred Revolt: the Muskogees' Struggle for a New World* (Boston: Beacon Press, 1991).

24. Anthony F. C. Wallace, *Jefferson and the Indians: the Tragic Fate of the First Americans* (Cambridge, MA: Belknap Press of Harvard University Press, 1999).

25. See the Supreme Court decisions *Johnson & Graham's Lessee v. M'Intosh* (1823), *Cherokee v. Georgia* (1831) and *Worcester v. Georgia* (1832).

26. Thurman Wilkins, *Cherokee Tragedy: The Ridge Family and the Decimation of a People* (2nd edn, Norman: University of Oklahoma Press, 1986); Michael D. Green, *The Politics of Indian Removal: Creek Government and Society in Crisis* (Lincoln: University of Nebraska Press, 1982); Jeremiah Evarts, *Cherokee Removal: The 'William Penn' Essays and Other Writings*, ed. Francis Paul Prucha (Knoxville: University of Tennessee, 1981); Clara Sue Kidwell, *Choctaws and Mississionaries in Mississippi 1818–1918* (Norman: University of Oklahoma Press, 1995).

27. Wilkins, *Cherokee Tragedy*, p. xiii.

28. John R. Finger, *The Eastern Band of Cherokees 1819–1900* (Knoxville: University of Tennessee Press, 1981); John R. Finger, *Cherokee Americans: The Eastern Band of Cherokees in the Twentieth Century* (Knoxville: University of Tennessee Press, 1984); Sharlotte Neely, *Snowbird Cherokees: People of Persistence* (Athens: University of Georgia Press, 1991); J. Anthony Paredes (ed.), *Indians of the Southeastern United States in the Late Twentieth Century* (Tuscaloosa: University of Alabama Press, 1992); Karen I. Blu, *The Lumbee Problem: The Making of an American Indian People* (Cambridge: Cambridge University Press, 1980); Gerald M. Sider, *Lumbee Indian Histories: Race, Ethnicity, and Indian Identity in the Southern United States* (Cambridge: Cambridge University Press, 1993); Rachel A. Bonney and J. Anthony Paredes (eds), *Anthropologists and Indians in the New South* (Tuscaloosa: University of Alabama Press, 2001).

29. Annie Heloise Abel, *Events Leading to the Consolidation of American Indian Tribes West of the Mississippi River*, Annual Report of the American Historical Association, 1906.

30. Douglas C. Jones, *The Treaty of Medicine Lodge, 1867* (Norman: University of Oklahoma Press, 1966).

31. Bernard W. Sheehan, *Seeds of Extinction: Jeffersonian Philanthropy and the American Indian* (Chapel Hill: published for the Institute of Early American History and Culture at Williamsburg, VA by the University of North Carolina Press, 1973); H. Craig Miner and William E. Unrau, *The End of Indian Kansas: A Study of Cultural Revolution, 1854–1871* (Lawrence: The Regents Press of Kansas, 1978).

32. D. S. Otis, *The Dawes Act and the Allotment of Indian Lands*, ed. by Francis Paul Prucha (Norman: University of Oklahoma Press, 1973); Wilcomb E. Washburn, *The Assault on Indian Tribalism: The General Allotment Law (Dawes Act) of 1887* (Philadelphia: Lippincott, 1975).

33. Angie Debo, *And Still the Waters Run* (New York: Gordian Press, 1966).

34. David Wallace Adams, *Education for Extinction* (Lawrence: University Press of Kansas, 1995); K. Tsianina Lomawaima, *They Called it Prairie Light: The Story of Chilocco Indian School* (Lincoln: University of Nebraska Press, 1994); Brenda Child, *Boarding School Seasons: American Indian Families, 1900–1940* (Lincoln: University of Nebraska Press, 1998); Clyde Ellis, *To Change Them Forever: Indian Education at the Rainy Mountain Boarding School, 1893–1920* (Norman: University of Oklahoma Press, 1996).

35. Frederick E. Hoxie, *A Final Promise: The Campaign to Assimilate the Indians, 1880–1920* (Lincoln: University of Nebraska Press, 1984).

36. Louis Merriam et al., *The Problem of Indian Administration* (Baltimore: Johns Hopkins Press, 1928).

37. William T. Hagan, *American Indians* (Chicago: University of Chicago Press, 1961).

38. Vine Deloria, Jr and Clifford M. Lytle, *The Nations Within: The Past and Future of American Indian Sovereignty* (New York: Pantheon Books, 1984).

39. Alison R. Bernstein, *American Indians and World War II: Toward a New Era in Indian Affairs* (Norman: University of Oklahoma Press, 1991).

40. Donald L. Fixico, *Termination and Relocation: Federal Indian Policy, 1945–1960* (Albuquerque: University of New Mexico Press, 1986); Kenneth R. Philp, *Termination Revisited: American Indians on the Trail to Self-Determination, 1933–1953* (Lincoln: University of Nebraska Press, 1999).

41. Joan Weibel-Orlando, *Indian Country, L.A.: Maintaining Ethnic Community in Complex Society* (Urbana: University of Illinois Press, 1991); *Urban Voices: The Bay Area American Indian Community*, Community History Project, Intertribal Friendship House, Oakland, California, ed. Susan Lobo (Tucson: University of Arizona Press, 2002).

42. Vine Deloria Jr, *Custer Died for your Sins* (London: Macmillan, 1969), p. 72.

43. Troy Johnson, Joane Nagel, and Duane Champagne (eds), *American Indian Activism: Alcatraz to the Longest Walk*, (Urbana: University of Illinois Press, 1997); Adam Fortunate Eagle, *Alcatraz! Alcatraz! The Indian Occupation of 1969–1971* (Berkeley, CA: Heyday Books, 1992).

44. Paul Chaat Smith and Robert Allen Warrior, *Like a Hurricane: The American Indian Movement from Alcatraz to Wounded Knee* (New York: New Press, 1996).

45. Vine Deloria, Jr, *Indians of the Pacific Northwest from the Coming of the White Man to the Present Day* (New York: Doubleday, 1977).

46. Devon Mihesuah (ed.), *Natives and Academics: Researching and Writing about American Indians* (Lincoln: University of Nebraska Press, 1998).

47. Clara Sue Kidwell, *Choctaws and Missionaries in Mississippi 1818–1918* (Norman: University of Oklahoma Press, 1995).

48. Sergei Kan, *Memory Eternal: Tlingit Culture and Russian Orthodox Christianity through Two Centuries* (Seattle: University of Washington Press, 1999); Loretta Fowler, *Tribal Sovereignty and the Historical Imagination: Cheyenne-Arapaho Politics* (Lincoln: University of Nebraska Press, 2002).

49. Jace Weaver, *That the People Might Live: Native American Literatures and Native American Community* (New York: Oxford University Press, 1997).

50. Patricia Nelson Limerick, *The Legacy of Conquest: the Unbroken Past of the American West* (New York: W. W. Norton, 1987); Richard White, *'It's Your Misfortune and None of My Own': A History of the American West* (Norman: University of Oklahoma Press, 1991).

CHAPTER 4

Tribal Sovereignty

The sovereignty of American Indian tribes is a function of their original occupation of the United States as self-governing entities. It is an inherent right, although the Congress of the United States has maintained at times that it was merely delegated to tribes by the federal government. The sovereign rights exercised by tribes in contemporary society include the right to determine membership, the right to tax their members, the right to regulate internal civil and criminal matters, and the right of sovereign immunity.[1] American Indian tribes are unique and individual groups, although the federal government has at times acted on the assumption that Indians constituted a racial group. The Supreme Court case of *Morton v. Mancari, 417 US 535 (1974)* affirmed the Indian preference policy of the Bureau of Indian Affairs in the face of federal laws against racial discrimination. The decision was based on racially-based hiring as a tool for carrying out federal policy, but it was important because it affirmed the special status of Indians before the law.

Politically, American Indians have a unique relationship with the federal government based on the treaties that they made as sovereign nations, first with the European colonizing powers and then with the United States. American Indians can argue that their governments predate the United States Constitution, and that their sovereign powers cannot be constrained by the federal government, although the form of many contemporary tribal governments was dictated by the United States under the Indian Reorganization Act of 1934.

Tribal sovereignty is a basic concept for Native American Studies, and the unique, fiduciary responsibility that the United States has toward

Indian tribes is an essential aspect of political identity for Indian people in the United States today. Sovereignty is a concept of which the meaning has been continually negotiated throughout the history of contact with European colonizers because, although it is held to be an inherent right, its political effect depends upon its recognition by other sovereigns.

Tribes initially signed treaties from positions of power as European governments attempted to establish their claims to new lands for settlement and wealth. The balance of power shifted as diseases took their toll on Native populations, and as Europeans came in increasing numbers to occupy the land. The status of Indian tribes as sovereign entities has changed over time, and it continues to evolve in contemporary society. The basic premise of sovereignty is, however, accepted as a given in Native American Studies.[2]

A corollary premise is that cultural integrity is integrally related to sovereignty. This is a political and social construct rather than a legal one. Cultural continuity is a requirement for federal recognition for tribes, but once a tribe is recognized, it is not compelled to demonstrate continuing culture. Politically however, if American Indians cannot demonstrate their cultural distinctiveness within American society, Congress can simply terminate its government-to-government relationships with tribes and deny their sovereignty, as happened during the termination era of the 1950s. If Indians look, act, talk, and live like all other Americans, Congress can simply cease to recognize that they exercise sovereign rights. Attempts by states to tax American Indians or to reduce federal appropriations for services when tribes are economically successful are examples of on-going attacks on the basic principles of tribal sovereignty.

Loss of federal recognition would not mean the end of tribal sovereignty per se, since tribes assert their sovereignty as an inherent right rather than one delegated by the US government. In the case of *Menominee Tribe v. United States, 391 U.S. 404 (1968)* the US Supreme Court held that tribal treaty rights to hunt and fish on certain lands remained despite the termination of the tribal government. Tribes could indeed continue to govern themselves without federal recognition. Any small, rural community that elects a mayor, city councilmen, and justices of the peace and has the power to regulate the behavior of its citizens, for example, has a degree of sovereignty, but it is delegated by the state. Tribes could maintain their governments, but they would be subject to the powers of state and local governments in a way that they are not with their special status vis à vis the US government.

There is an inherent tension in the concept of sovereignty between the idea of federal responsibility toward tribes as defined in treaty relations, and the assertion by tribes that they are not subject to federal power. Treaties give tribes the right to call upon the federal government for protection and services, in exchange for which tribes have generally given up land and committed themselves to loyalty to the United States. Treaty obligations and notions of inherent sovereignty reside uneasily together. This tension has revealed itself in different ways over time. From John Marshall's decisions in the 1830s, in which he acknowledged the rights of tribes to govern their own internal affairs, through the decision in *Lone Wolf v. Hitchcock* in 1903, which established the doctrine of the plenary power of Congress over Indians, to assertions by contemporary US Congressmen that tribes are simply voluntary political organizations, the relationship between tribes and the US government has been the subject of constant negotiation and evolving ideas about what constitutes tribal identity.[3]

THE TRADE AND INTERCOURSE ACTS

Under the terms of treaties that promised that the US government would protect Indian lands from invasion by non-Indians, Congress began regulating the actions of US citizens in relation to Indians, thus preempting state power to do so. It also established a basic jurisdictional principle that the federal government regulated its citizens, and Indian tribes regulated the behavior of their citizens. The first of a series of Trade and Intercourse acts was passed in 1790. An important area of this regulation involved the Indian trade. As with colonial governments, it behooved the United States to maintain peaceful and fair relationships between traders and Indians in order to promote the trade. The Act required traders to acquire licenses before they could enter Indian territory, and prohibited the introduction of alcohol. The original Trade and Intercourse act was made permanent in 1834 after being renewed by Congress on a regular basis until then.[4] It remained in force until late in the nineteenth century.

THE MARSHALL TRILOGY

The decisions of Supreme Court Justice John Marshall, the so-called 'Marshall trilogy,' are cited as the basis for the fiduciary relationship

between the tribes and the US government. The unique historical relationship of tribes to the US government was first defined in these decisions. In
the broader historical picture, Marshall's decisions collectively established
important principles in defining the general power of the judiciary branch
of the US government with respect to the legislative and executive
branches.[5] Marshall's decisions were also made in the political context of
the struggle between states' rights and the powers of the federal government, a struggle that has been a recurrent theme in American history and
is increasingly a theme in contemporary issues of tribes vis à vis the states.

In 1823, in the case of *Johnson and Graham's Lessee v. M'Intosh, 21 U.S.
(8 Wheat.) 543 (1823)*, the basic question was to establish the ownership of
land, originally granted to Englishmen by Indians in the 1770s, that the
United States claimed as descended from the colonial claims of the British
government. Marshall established the so-called 'Doctrine of Discovery,'
asserting that Indians had only rights of occupancy rather than full title to
their lands according to American legal concepts. Title lay with those who
discovered the land, and only they could sell it. Marshall's corollary
'Doctrine of Conquest' laid the basis for the historical dispossession of
Indians of their lands by asserting the power of a conquerer to take land
from the conquered.

In the case of *Cherokee Nation v. Georgia* in 1830, the Cherokee Nation
challenged the right of the state of Georgia to extend its laws over the
Cherokee Nation, and Marshall ruled that Indian Nations, as designated in
the US Constitution, were unique entities, now dependent on the government for protection, like 'a ward to its guardian.' This decision formalized
the fiduciary or trust relationship between tribes and the US government.
This unique relationship, however, meant that the Supreme Court could
not hear a suit because its jurisdiction extended only over cases involving
states and foreign governments. The Cherokees were neither.

The final decision involved a challenge to the authority of the state of
Georgia to exercise its laws in the Cherokee Nation. Samuel Worcester was
arrested and imprisoned by the state of Georgia for preaching in the
Cherokee Nation without a permit from the state. He brought a suit charg-
ing that the state did not have the right to extend its laws over the Nation.
In *Worcester v. Georgia (1831)*, John Marshall asserted that the responsibility for dealing with American Indians was a federal one, guaranteed in the
Constitution. He affirmed the primacy of federal jurisdiction over state
jurisdiction and the unique relationship between Indian tribes and the
federal government.[6]

All three of Marshall's decisions acknowledged the rights of tribes to govern their own internal civil affairs. It was in their relationships to white society and to the federal government that they were seen as helpless and in need of protection. The fiduciary relationship implies that the guardian will make choices for the best interest of the ward, but as has proven the case throughout the history of Indian-white relations, what the guardian interprets as 'best interest' may differ significantly from the interpretation of the ward. This tension between paternalism and responsibility is evident throughout the history of the relationship between tribes and the federal government. Tribes can call upon the government to honor treaty relationships by providing services promised in those agreements, at the same time that they insist upon their right to maintain the integrity of their own governments.

Indian Nations, however, were faced with the prospect of maintaining their sovereignty at the expense of their tribal lands in the east as Andrew Jackson pushed the Indian Removal Act through Congress in 1830. The act provided that the tribes would exchange their eastern lands for lands west of the Mississippi River and move there. Treaties with the Cherokees, Choctaws, Chickasaws, Creeks, and Seminoles, the so-called 'civilized' tribes who had accepted Christian missionary schools and churches, expressed both the desire of the tribes to maintain their own governments and the promises of the United States to protect their new lands west of the Mississippi from invasion by non-Indians. In 1834, the federal government passed the last of the Indian Trade and Intercourse acts, formalizing the federal Office of Indian Affairs as the body in the executive branch to regulate those relationships.[7]

The process of treaty making through the mid-nineteenth century was increasingly coercive as white settlers moved into Indian lands. The transfer of the Bureau of Indian Affairs from the Department of War to the Department of the Interior in 1849 was a symbolic declaration by the US government that Indian resistance was at an end and that the resources of Indian land were now available for exploitation.[8] The Gold Rush of 1848 inspired westward movement. Major treaties at Fort Wise (1851), Fort Atkinson (1861), Medicine Lodge (1867), and Fort Laramie (1868) served to define the land bases of Plains tribes and to reinforce the terminology of dependency of tribes on the federal government.[9]

The Civil War had an enormous impact on the Five Tribes in Indian Territory. Abandoned by the US government, which withdrew its forces as the Confederacy invaded Indian Territory, they signed treaties with the

Confederacy at the start of the war, and the defeat of the Confederacy forced them into new treaties that redefined their relationship to the United States. Although their rights of self-government were recognized, they were forced to cede certain lands to the US government, to admit their freed slaves as citizens of their nations, and to grant rights of way for railroads across their territory.[10]

The completion of the transcontinental railroad in 1869 symbolized the final opening of Indian land to American desire. In 1871, the US government abandoned its practice of making treaties with Indian tribes. Reservations of land and agreements with tribes continued through executive orders by the President of the United States and acts of Congress, but the formality of treaties that acknowledged Indian sovereignty was now a dead letter. Increasingly, legal decisions defined Indian rights.[11] Boarding schools removed Indian children from their homes and contributed to the loss of Indian cultures as children were forbidden to speak their languages, and were not allowed to go home to participate in ceremonial activities.[12]

In 1883, the case of *ex parte Crow Dog* set a new legal precedent. Coming as it did during the general era of Indian policy calling for allotment of land to individual Indians and the dissolution of tribal government, the decision of the Supreme Court in *ex parte Crow Dog* came to the heart of the challenge that Indian sovereignty posed to federal power. When Crow Dog shot his fellow tribesman Spotted Tail on the Brule Lakota (Sioux) reservation in 1883, he was punished by the tribe by having to make restitution to Spotted Tail's kinsmen, but he was also seized and tried in a territorial court and convicted. He appealed to the Supreme Court of the United States, which refused jurisdiction on the grounds that the crime had been committed by Indians on an Indian reservation and was thus a matter for the tribe to settle.[13]

The Court, by allowing a murderer to be left to the jurisdiction of his own people, to be punished as they chose, thus affirmed tribal sovereignty. The Congress of the United States, however, reacting to this perceived affront to American moral values, proceeded to pass the Major Crimes Act in 1885, declaring that the United States had jurisdiction over crimes committed in lands reserved to Indian tribes. The extent of US jurisdiction was tested in 1886 in the case of *US v. Kagama*, arising as before out of the killing of one Indian by another on the Humboldt reservation in California. The US Supreme Court accepted the case, thereby establishing a precedent that acts of Congress vis à vis Indian tribes were subject to judicial review as to their constitutionality.

The relationship between tribes and the federal government under the Constitution rests in a single phrase in Article 1, Section 8, governing commerce between the United States and Indian tribes. In a wonderfully convoluted example of legal reasoning in the *Kagama* case, federal attorneys argued that if Indians were killing each other, that situation inhibited the ability of the United States to carry out commerce with the Indians because there were fewer of them to engage in trade.[14] The case thus brought tribes within the purview of the United States Constitution, contravening the fact that tribal governments far preceded the Constitution, and compromising their independent status. This principle of judicial review has become important in the twentieth century as the Supreme Court in the mid-century upheld principles of tribal sovereignty in many of its decisions.[15]

In 1903, the Supreme Court asserted the power of Congress to abrogate Indian treaties in the case of *Lone Wolf v. Hitchcock*, a suit brought by the Kiowa tribe against the Secretary of the Interior. The issue was a treaty provision requiring a vote of at least three-fourths of tribal members before any changes in the treaty could be made. The Supreme Court ruled that the dependency of tribes on the federal government meant that the Congress could decide what was best for the tribes, even if it meant setting aside treaty provisions.[16]

The late nineteenth and early twentieth centuries marked the nadir of tribal sovereignty as the United States government passed the General Allotment Act in 1887, also known as the Dawes Act after its sponsor, Senator Henry Dawes of Massachusetts, a man deeply involved with the social reform movements that characterized the late nineteenth and early twentieth centuries. Indian values of communal property clashed directly with a deeply held American belief in the value of private property, which included a belief in its ability to instill values of thrift, industry, and self-sufficiency in its holders. The Dawes Act provided for the allotment of reservation lands in individual plots of 160 acres to heads of families, eighty acres to single persons over eighteen years of age and to orphans, and forty acres to single persons under eighteen. Title to the land was restricted for twenty-five years, that is, the owner could not sell during that period. These restrictions were intended to protect the land while Indians learned to farm and become self-sufficient.[17]

Several of the tribes in Indian Territory (what is now the state of Oklahoma) – the Cherokees, Choctaws, Chickasaws, Creeks and Seminoles (known as the Five Civilized Tribes), Osages, Sac and Foxes, Miamis, Peorias, and Senecas – were exempt from the act for various reasons. For the Five Civilized Tribes, it was because their treaties in the 1830s had given them patents in fee simple (that is, full legal title), to their lands. Nevertheless, the continued existence of the Indian Territory as an area outside the legal jurisdiction of the United States was anathema to many members of Congress, and in 1889 an act was passed that extended limited civil and criminal jurisdiction over Indian Territory, thereby making Indians subject to legal action in their dealings with whites (25 Stat. 783).[18]

In 1893 Congress empowered a three-person Commission, chaired by Henry Dawes, to go to Indian Territory to persuade the Five Civilized Tribes to accept allotment of land and a Territorial government and ultimate statehood. After difficult and protracted negotiations, the Commission signed agreements with the tribes providing for allotment of their lands and the ultimate dissolution of their tribal governments. The Curtis Act, passed on 28 June 1898, laid out the terms for allotment and ratified the agreements with the Choctaws, Chickasaws and Creeks. Subsequent agreements were made with the Cherokees and Seminoles.[19]

Although the Dawes Act provided for a twenty-five year trust period, in 1906 Congress passed the Burke Act (24 Stat. 182) which allowed the Secretary of the Interior to grant fee patents to Indians whom he decided were competent to manage their own affairs. Through this mechanism many Indians received title to their lands and subsequently sold them or lost them because they did not pay taxes.

The implementation of the Dawes Act and the Curtis Act has significant implications for contemporary tribal membership. The compilation of rolls of tribal members was a necessary prerequisite for the distribution of tribal lands. Those rolls have become the basis for determining current membership in many tribes. For the Five Tribes, degree of Indian blood was noted on the enrollment cards, reifying distinctions between full bloods, half bloods, quarter bloods, and so on. With regard to land, an act in 1908 (35 Stat. L., 312) provided that Indians of less than half blood would have all restrictions on their lands removed. The Act also lifted restrictions on land after the death of an allottee, meaning that heirs (except minor children) were free to sell the land. The Secretary of the Interior also had the power to lift restrictions based on his judgment of competency. Not only did the Curtis Act provide for the end of tribal sovereignty for the Five Tribes, but the Act of 1908 reified the idea of blood quantum, with the result that members of the Five Tribes lost significant amounts of their lands.[20]

The assault on tribal sovereignty was reversed temporarily in 1934 with the passage of the Indian Reorganization Act, which stopped the allotment process and allowed tribes to organize their own governments, albeit in forms suggested by the Bureau of Indian Affairs to replicate the United States Constitution.[21] Although the act reasserted a form of self-government, it contained a strong element of fostering economic self-sufficiency that, implicitly, would lead the way to the termination of the federal-tribal relationships.[22] This reassertion of tribal sovereignty came under harsh attack in 1943 as a result of the cost-cutting mentality of the federal government during the Second World War, and in the post-war era the general national prosperity made it appear that Indians would be able to assimilate into American society. The termination policy was explicated in a Congressional action, Joint Resolution 108, in 1953.[23] Secretary of the Interior Fred Zimmerman was asked to draw up a list of tribes that met certain criteria – their ability to sustain themselves economically, their acceptance by their non-Indian neighbors, and their ability to interact with non-Indians.[24] The attempt to terminate the relationship with tribes was finally repudiated by President Richard Nixon in 1970, and in 1973 the American Indian Policy Review Commission was established by Congress to investigate the status of the American Indian tribes. The Final Report of the Commission began with a very strong assertion of the inherent sovereignty of American Indian tribes. Congressman Lloyd Meeds from the state of Washington, and a member of the Commission, issued a strong dissent from the position of the Committee, objecting to the concept of tribal sovereignty, but Congress passed the Indian Self-Determination and Educational Improvement Act of 1975 (88 Stat. 2203).[25] Nixon's repudiation of the termination policy, and the passage of the Self Determination Act established the basis for the current federal recognition of sovereignty, that is, the ability of tribes to contract for federal funds to run their own social service programs.[26]

Debates over the nature of tribal identity are an underlying theme in discussions of tribal sovereignty. Identity has many markers, both among those who are members of a tribe, and to those looking at the tribe from the outside. Native people today are descendents of peoples who lived in what is now the United States long before Europeans began to settle there. Native people can thus argue that their identity is inherent and descends from their autochthonous ancestors, no matter how remote. In contemporary society, however, the dilution of blood and the effects of federal policies have stripped many communities and individuals of language, ceremonies, and obvious phenotypical difference.[27]

As sovereign entities, tribes exercise their own power to determine who are members of the group. This right of determining membership is generally deemed one of the powers of any sovereign government, and it has been upheld by the United States Supreme Court in the case of *Santa Clara Pueblo v. Martinez, 436 U.S. 49 (1978)*, in which a female tribal member married to a Navajo man challenged the right of the Pueblo government to pass a law that membership depended upon the father. Mrs Martinez's children were not eligible for tribal membership even though they lived in the Pueblo and were raised culturally as Pueblo, but the Supreme Court affirmed the tribal ordinance.[28]

In contemporary society, Indian identity may simply be represented by the possession of a Certificate of Degree of Indian Blood (CDIB), issued by the Bureau of Indian Affairs and based on descent from a federally approved roll of original tribal members compiled in the late nineteenth century. Tribes generally require a CDIB before they will issue a tribal enrollment card. Of all ethnic groups in the United States, only American Indians must produce documentary proof of lineage and make a conscious effort to be identified as members of federally recognized tribes. Tribes use blood quantum, that is, biological descent, as the most common criterion for membership.[29] The arbitrariness of this process is again a function of federal policy, because descent is generally determined from an ancestor on a roll compiled in the late 1890s as part of carrying out the allotment of Indian land. It has, however, led to challenges to tribal sovereignty on the grounds that tribes are voluntary political associations rather than unique Indian communities.

Throughout the historical process, the concept of sovereignty has changed – from one of the inherent sovereignty of aboriginal nations in their original homes, to the contested sovereignty of contemporary tribes that pits tribal, state, and federal governments against each other. A major issue in contemporary society is the on-going political tension between federal and state rights, which has complicated the federal-tribal relationship since tribal reservations and trust land are within the boundaries of states.

CONTEMPORARY ISSUES IN TRIBAL SOVEREIGNTY

The issues that confront tribes today are rooted in the historical past, but they reflect the current reality of the status of American Indians as a very small population within American society. According to the 2000 census, American Indians constitute 0.08 per cent of the American population.

Jurisdiction and land ownership

Jurisdiction is an essential element of sovereignty. The power of a government to govern its citizens derives from its power to control a land base. This power reflects back to our initial premise about the cultural association of Native people to their lands. In modern legal parlance, however, it depends on the ability of tribal groups to control lands that have been fragmented as a result of the federal policy of allotment. The concept of Indian Country was formalized in law in 1948. Indian Country comprises

(a) all land within the limits of any Indian reservation under the jurisdiction of the United States Government, notwithstanding the issuance of any patent, and, including rights-of-way running through the reservation, (b) all dependent Indian communities within the borders of the United States whether within the original or subsequently acquired territory thereof, and whether within or without the limits of a state, and (c) all Indian allotments, the Indian titles to which have not been extinguished, including rights-of-way running through the same. (18 USC 1151)[30]

The issue of jurisdiction is also complicated by the fragmented land holdings in tribal areas. The allotment process essentially froze tribal land holdings at the time that tribal rolls were closed. Children born after the closing could only inherit rather than claim land in their own right. Complicated laws of probate and guardianship and the instability of life in many reservation communities led to increasingly fractionated holdings of tribal land. This legacy of federal policy encouraging private land ownership has effectively removed significant tracts of Indian land from any effective use, and has contributed to administrative chaos in the administration of payments to heirs for income from their lands.

The government's inability to account for possibly billions of dollars of income due to Indians from leases of coal, oil, timber, and grazing rights has led to a lawsuit originally filed in 1996. The case of *Cobell v. Babbitt (91 f. Supp. 2d at 34)* has in turn led to judgments of contempt of court against federal officials, exposure of totally incompetent record keeping with regard to individual Indian trust accounts, shutdown of the Bureau of Indian Affairs Internet site, and a seemingly irresolvable situation in which incomplete records make it impossible to know exactly how much income is due to individual Indian land holders. Congressional attempts to allow Indian

Nations to recover lands from the estates of deceased individuals have been thwarted by a Supreme Court holding in *Babbitt, Secretary of Interior, et al., v. Youpee, et al.* (1997) upholding the sanctity of the rights of private owners.[31] The main recourse available to Indian tribes is to sue for land under historical treaty rights. Given the past federal policy of removing Indians from their homelands by negotiating treaties that called for their removal to other places, the field seems open for reclaiming those original lands where the federal government did not honor its part of the agreement, but these arguments are based in complex historical relationships and the differing understandings of treaty language, which was often frustratingly vague. Although John Marshall established a principal that treaty language must be interpreted in favor of Indian tribes where there was any ambiguity, courts have not always been lenient in that regard.

Tribal Courts

Tribal jurisdiction involves some system for making decisions. Tribal traditions of clan and family-based retribution have given way to more formal tribal court systems, although some tribes have integrated elements of arbitration as settlement.[32] The Indian Civil Rights Act in 1968 extended the provisions of the Bill of Rights to Indian tribes, with certain modifications to allow for theocratic forms of government among the Pueblos and the operations of tribal courts. It restricted those operations by limiting the amount of fines and the lengths of sentences they could impose, and limiting their ability to hold prisoners for criminal offenses. It imposed restrictions on the right of tribes to govern themselves by requiring tribal governments to adopt a set of laws that largely replicated the Bill of Rights. Despite the limitations, the Supreme Court affirmed tribal sovereignty by upholding the decision of the tribal court in *Santa Clara Pueblo v. Martinez* in 1968.[33]

Taxation

The power to tax is an element of sovereignty. In American society the public sector (that is, governments) collect taxes from the private sector (that is, individual wage earners, entrepreneurs, and property owners). Taxes support the government so that it can provide services to its citizens. The concept of taxation was unknown in communal tribal societies, which were based on social obligations of reciprocity structured by kinship systems, and chiefs assumed responsibility for those in the society (widows, orphans) who had no kin to support them. The well-being of individuals was the concern of extended families. In contemporary society, tribal governments provide services for their members – educational programs, nutrition programs for expectant mothers and the elderly, healthcare – largely through federally funded programs which they contract to operate under the Indian Self-Determination and Educational Improvement Act of 1975.

If the power to tax is an essential part of governance, it also raises unique issues for Indian tribes. If tribes impose taxes on tribal members to support their operations, will the federal government find reason to reduce funding for programs that Indians feel are based on treaty obligations? Indian land is not subject to taxation by states or the federal government, and Indians working on Indian land do not pay state income taxes. Tribes have developed enterprises on tribal land that are exempt from state taxation – primarily sales of tobacco products and gasoline. The fact that these products encourage non-Indian consumers to buy from tribes rather than private businesses exacerbates the tension between states and tribes. Indian land is encompassed in state land. The tax exemptions that tribes enjoy have been a major point of contention between tribal and state governments.[34]

The issue of taxation points up the conflict between states and tribes, and the larger states' rights issues that have been continually contested between the federal government and states. The state of Oklahoma, for instance, has consistently challenged the exemption of tribes (whose very existence has been at issue since 1907 when the Indian Territory in eastern Oklahoma was joined with Oklahoma Territory to form the new state) from state taxes.[35]

Economic Development

The policy of the United States government in the late nineteenth century was to impose individual ownership of land to encourage economic self-sufficiency. In the twentieth century, beginning with the Indian Reorganization Act, the government embarked on an explicit policy to make tribes economically self-sufficient in the wage-based, capitalistic economy of modern America. This shift in policy has introduced a new set of issues into American Indians' traditional relationship to their homelands.

Gaming

The Indian Gaming Regulatory Act of 1988 (IGRA) demonstrates most pointedly the complex issues of Indian self-government, federal policy, and state interests. The Cabezon Rancheria in California took advantage of its exemption from state laws to offer bingo games with stakes far beyond those regulated by the states. The Supreme Court ruled in favor of the tribe's ability to operate its own games. The prospect of tribes earning significant income from gaming operations raised questions of federal jurisdiction, and Congress passed the act to assert its control over tribal gaming operations. Indeed, IGRA is more comprehensive over every aspect of the management of Indian gaming than any other federal or state legislation. The extraordinary detail of the act was inspired in large part by the fear among federal legislators that organized criminal groups would attempt to profit from Indian gaming activities. The preamble to IGRA is, however, explicit in its intent to encourage Indian economic development, but the act is also problematic in its provisions that restrict gaming to agreements with states for the conduct of gaming. These compacts have given rise to a kind of de facto state taxation of tribes through tribal agreements to pay percentages of their gaming profits to states. Tribes retain the ability to determine how gaming income is used, but if it is distributed to tribal members, it becomes subject to state and federal taxation.[36] Annual reports of gaming revenues show incredibly large profits for some tribes that are located near urban areas, while small-scale operations in rural areas produce little economic benefit to tribal communities. Although gaming has brought economic benefit and concomitant political power to some tribes, it also raises a host of issues with regard to the ability of tribes to govern their own affairs, their relationship with states, and their subjection to federal and state taxation.

Water Rights

In the arid western part of the United States, beyond the Mississippi River, where most tribal reservations are located, water is a precious commodity, as it has been since American settlers moved into the area. Since control of land is the province of a sovereign government, control of its resources is also essential to sovereignty. When the federal government signed treaties with tribes, it generally relegated them to the most remote and seemingly unproductive parts of what had originally been rich hunting grounds. Those lands proved, in the late nineteenth and early twentieth centuries, to be rich in coal, oil, gold, and other minerals. Mining depended upon water, as did the development of the land for agriculture.

In contemporary society, water rights are important both for tribal self-sufficiency and economic development. The precedent for Indian water rights is the Supreme Court decision in the *Winters* case involving the Milk River in Montana in 1908 (*Winters v. United States, 207 US 564*) The instance of the suit was the damming of the Milk River in 1900 in a way that cut off its flow to the Fort Belknap Indian Reservation. The government sued the dam owners, arguing that the tribe had rights of prior appropriation of the water. This right of prior appropriation is a governing principle in water rights law in the west. Despite the precedent of the Winters doctrine, competing claims by non-Indians have consistently challenged Indian rights. Water rights are regulated by state laws, and the rights of tribes as federal entities come into conflict with the rights of individuals who seek to use water for economic interests, particularly in the arid west. The main issue with regard to water rights involves their very determination. Various treaties providing for the development of reservation land in the west promised the amount of water that Indians would need to cultivate their land. Water is, however, an increasingly limited resource, and dividing it according to the needs of various users is problematic. Tribes must either agree to subject the issue to the quantification of a specific volume of water or to stand by their rights of prior appropriation of undetermined amounts of water.[37] If tribes agree to quantification, they could be assured of rights to specific amounts of water, but they may forfeit rights that would be possible in future situations. If they do not agree, they face the prospect of litigation that could drag on for years (as it has in many cases) as their federally determined rights conflict with the rights of states. The decisions that tribes face with regard to water rights represent a new challenge to sovereignty. Although the principles of the Winters doctrine give them a theoretical right, political realities in the modern world challenge them to decide what is in the best interests of the tribe in a litigious society.

Cultural Issues

Although sovereignty is generally considered a political issue, it is also deeply embedded in culture, that is, the association between sovereignty and cultural integrity. In 1978 the federal government passed the American Indian Religious Freedom Act, which, despite its name, did nothing more than direct federal agencies to examine their policies and procedures in order to determine whether they were contravening American Indian religious practices.

The act was important because Native religions are based in association with the land, and treaties and federal policy had taken many of the places where humans could communicate with the spiritual world out of the control of tribes. Sites of traditional vision quests where men sought spiritual power have generally become parts of national parks and forests because of their unusual aspect and physical beauty. Indian people recognized their distinctive features as sources of spiritual power. Protection of sacred sites is an essential aspect of tribal sovereignty, but it is also one of the most contentious because it pits tribal rights to freedom of religious expression as both a cultural issue and a first amendment issue under the US Constitution against federal issues of the greater good of American society. Because Indian religions are based in their association with land, which is generally beyond their legal control, when they seek exclusive rights to use public lands for religious use, issues concerning Indian religious practice and use of land come into direct conflict with the notion that public lands exist to be used for the benefit of the American public.[38]

Two court cases decided by the Supreme Court in 1988 have become touchstones for the issues of religious freedom in the twenty-first century. The case of *Lyng v. Northwest Indian Cemetery Protective Association* resulted in a Supreme Court decision that the greater economic good of American society meant that a logging company had the right to build a road through forest areas where the 'doctors' of the Tolowa, Yokuts, and Karok tribes went to seek their spiritual powers.[39]

The case of *Employment Division v. Smith* in 1990 reinforced the premise that the greater good of the American public overrode Indian rights to traditional religious practices.[40] At issue was the use of peyote by members of the Native American Church, a legally incorporated religion that had been established in 1918 to protect a new form of Native religion that had arisen in response to the suppression of the Ghost Dance and the Sun Dance by government agents.

The Smith case was not an Indian issue. It rather affirmed the right of the state of Oregon to make laws for what it perceived as a greater public good and that contravened certain rights of religious freedom. It provoked significant response not only in Indian communities but a much wider response in non-Indian communities that led to further Congressional action and Supreme Court review. It also led the Congress of the United States to pass a law that protected the use of peyote by members of the Native American Church, thus establishing a federal precedent to override state laws.[41]

The essential nature of land for cultural identity has led the Choctaw Nation in Oklahoma to provide buses to transport tribal members in

Oklahoma to Tennessee to visit an archaeological site on the outskirts of Memphis that is associated with the tribal origins, and to Nanih Waiya, the mound in north-central Mississippi that is associated with the tribal origin tradition. Although issues of the use of land for spiritual purposes has become embroiled in the legal processes of American society, land and relation to certain physical sites are still a part of day-to-day identity for many Indian people.

Repatriation

The correlation between tribal sovereignty and cultural integrity is most apparent in the passage of the National Museum of the American Indian Act (20 USC 3, XIII) and the Native American Graves Protection and Repatriation Act of 1990 (25 USC 32). The NMAI Act mandated that the Smithsonian Institution in Washington would return Indian human remains and 'associated funerary objects,' (grave goods) to American Indian tribes. The Native American Graves Protection and Repatriation Act extended that mandate to all museums and repositories receiving federal funding, and also expanded the categories of objects to include sacred objects, unassociated funerary objects, and objects of 'cultural patrimony,' (that is, things that were held to be owned by the tribe as a whole and that could not be alienated from the tribal holding by any individual). These two acts create a federal mandate through which Native people can recover objects that are essential to their religious practices and their cultural identity.[42] They speak directly to the unique relationship between Indian tribes and the US government, since tribes have the right to present their claims, and to the relationship between tribal sovereignty and Indian culture.

Social Issues

American Indian identity is based primarily in families, and the assault on Native families in the twentieth century has been a major policy issue for tribes. The historical assault on Indian families was explicit in the nineteenth-century federal policy of sending children to boarding schools, where they were to be stripped of their tribal identity, forbidden to speak their tribal languages, and changed into models of American citizens. The boarding school policy had significant implications for Indian identity. Native languages declined as English became the common language of couples who met in boarding schools and married. Students indoctrinated in the assimilationist policy of the boarding school chose not to teach their languages to their children.

The American Indian Child Welfare Act

The policy of removing children from their homes extended into the twentieth century as state and federal social service agents exercised their discretion to remove children from what they perceived as unhealthy home situations, and to place them in non-Indian foster homes. The American Indian Child Welfare Act of 1978 asserted the right of Indian tribes to determine the placement of tribal children with Indian families rather than in non-Indian foster homes. The act reaffirmed the sovereign right of American Indian tribes to protect their children and give them a grounding in their own tribal cultures. The Supreme Court upheld that right in the case of *Mississippi Choctaw Indian Band v. Holyfield*, a case in which an unmarried Choctaw couple arranged for the birth of their twin children off the reservation and their adoption by a non-Indian couple. The court ruled that the American Indian Child Welfare Act created a jurisdictional situation that could not be thwarted by the parents' action, thus affirming the sovereign right of the tribal government to control the actions of its citizens.[43]

CONCLUSION

Sovereignty is an essential concept in Native American Studies programs. It is key to understanding the historical relationship of Indians to non-Indians, and it is critical to the future of tribes as recognizable entities in American society. It must be understood as a matter of identity, that is, the right of a tribe to define its own members and of members to identify themselves as tribal members. It is a political issue as tribes exercise their rights to self-government vis à vis federal, state, and local government with which they must interact.

Sovereignty is an idealistic construct, but in its practical application it is subject to constraints. Legally, Indians are subject to certain Congressional laws that are still in force: the Major Crimes Act, which currently extends federal jurisdiction over Indians charged with one or more of thirteen crimes named in the Act; the Indian Civil Rights Act, which puts limits on the terms and fines that tribal courts can levy, and offers the right of habeas corpus to persons held on charges in tribal jails; and the Indian Gaming

Regulatory Act, which subjects tribes to the necessity of bargaining with states if they wish to establish casinos. Federal law defines Indian country, with complex jurisdictional distinctions made on the basis of the race of the plaintiff and the defendant, and whether the crime occurred in Indian country or outside.

Although the Marshall decisions affirm the 'dependent, domestic nations' as dependent on the federal government, recent shifts in federal policy, including the Indian Gaming Regulatory Act and state challenges to the tax-exempt status of tribal business operations, raise the spectre of the federal government delegating its responsibility to state governments. The concept of sovereignty is under political attack on many fronts, and the struggle to protect it may also be a source of assertions of tribal identity.

The idea of a self-governing community, in a practical sense, is also often a matter of contention within groups. Tribal constitutions – the major systematic expression of sovereignty because they are subject to the approval of the Bureau of Indian Affairs according to the Bureau's policies – and tribal elections become contentious when factions within the community question their legitimacy. These internal struggles call attention to the fact that there may not be unanimous agreement on what is the legitimate government of a community. The idealistic call to responsibility to one's community often raises the question, who represents the community?

The heart of the concept of sovereignty is twofold: people, and land. The power of a government to control its land lay in a sense of communal property defined by its use for subsistence and spiritual purposes. In modern American society, tribal land often means control of economic resources – timber, minerals, grazing land, and water – and it is often the case, as in the Winters doctrine, that the perceived good of the general public comes into conflict with the treaty rights of Indian tribes, and that federal courts become the deciding ground in the resulting contest. Tribes must then decide between affirming abstract rights and engaging in prolonged litigation without the guarantee of a favorable judgment, or reaching negotiated settlements that assure that they receive a defined benefit from their resources.

In Native American/American Indian Studies programs, tribal sovereignty must be taught both as an ideal to be sustained, and one whose meaning is constantly under negotiation with states, in federal courts, and with the Congress of the United States.

NOTES

1. Felix S. Cohen, *Handbook of Federal American Indian Law* (Washington, DC: U.S. Government Printing Service, 1983), p. 122.
2. Rennard Strickland, 'The Eagle's Empire,' in Russell Thornton (ed.), *Studying Native America: Problems and Prospects* (Madison: University of Wisconsin Press, 1998).
3. Wilcomb E. Washburn, *Red Man's Land, White Man's Law* (Norman: University of Oklahoma Press, 1995; Blue Clark, *Lone Wolf v. Hitchcock: Treaty Rights and Indian Law at the End of the Nineteenth Century* (Lincoln and London: University of Nebraska Press, 1994); James A. Clifton, 'Michigan's Indians: Tribe, nation, estate, racial, ethnic, or special interest group?', *Michigan Historical Review*, 20: 2 (Fall, 1994), 93–152.
4. Francis Paul Prucha, *American Indian Policy in the Formative Years: The Indian Trade and Intercourse Acts 1780–1834* (Cambridge, MA: Harvard University Press, 1962).
5. David E. Wilkins and Vine Deloria, Jr, *Tribes, Trials, and Constitutional Tribulations* (Austin: University of Texas Press, 2000).
6. Washburn, *Red Man's Land*, pp. 68–9.
7. Francis Paul Prucha, *The Great Father: The United States Government and the American Indians* (Lincoln: University of Nebraska Press, 1986).
8. Brian W. Dippie, *The Vanishing American: White Attitudes and US Indian Policy* (Middletown, CT: Wesleyan University Press, 1982).
9. Douglas C. Jones, *The Treaty of Medicine Lodge; The Story of the Great Treaty Council as Told by Eyewitnesses* (Norman: University of Oklahoma Press, 1966); Robert A. Trennert, *Alternative to Extinction: Federal Indian Policy and the Beginnings of the Reservation System* (Philadelphia, PA: Temple University Press, 1975).
10. Annie Heloise Abel, *The American Indian and the End of the Confederacy, 1863–65* (Lincoln: University of Nebraska Press, 1992).
11. David E. Wilkins, *American Indian Sovereignty and the US Supreme Court: The Masking of Justice* (Austin: University of Texas Press, 1997); Charles F. Wilkinson, *American Indians, Time, and the Law: Native Societies in a Modern Constitutional Society* (New Haven: Yale University Press, 1988).
12. Brenda J. Child, *Boarding School Seasons: American Indian Families, 1900–1940* (Lincoln: University of Nebraska Press, 2000); Clyde Ellis, *To Change Them Forever: Indian Education at the Rainy Mountain Boarding School, 1893–1920* (Norman: University of Oklahoma Press, 1996); K. Tsianina. Lomawaima, *They Called It Prairie Light: The Story of Chilocco Indian School* (Lincoln: University of Nebraska Press, 1994); David W. Adams, *Education for Extinction: American Indians and the Boarding School Experience, 1875–1928* (Lawrence: University of Kansas Press, 1995).
13. Sidney L. Harring, *Crow Dog's Case: American Indian Sovereignty, Tribal Law, and United States Law in the Nineteenth Century* (New York: Cambridge University Press, 1994).
14. Wilkins, *American Indian Sovereignty*, pp. 70–1.
15. Wilkins, *American Indian Sovereignty*, pp. 2–5; Wilkinson, *American Indians*, pp. 1–6; Strickland, pp. 262–3.

16. Blue Clark, *Lone Wolf v. Hitchcock*.

17. D. S. Otis, *The Dawes Act and the Allotment of Indian Lands*, ed. Francis Paul Prucha (Norman: University of Oklahoma Press, 1973); Wilcomb E. Washburn, *The Assault on Indian Tribalism: The General Allotment Law (Dawes Act) of 1887* (Philadelphia: Lippincott, 1975); Grant Foreman, *The Five Civilized Tribes* (Norman: University of Oklahoma Press, 1934).

18. Jeffrey Burton, *Indian Territory and the United States, 1866–1906: Courts, Government, and the Movement for Oklahoma Statehood* (Norman and London: University of Oklahoma Press, 1995).

19. Kent Carter, *The Dawes Commission and the Allotment of the Five Civilized Tribes, 1893–1914* (Orem, UT: Ancestry.com, 1999).

20. Angie Debo, *And Still the Waters Run* (Princeton: Princeton University Press, 1940).

21. Lawrence C. Kelly, *The Assault on Assimilation : John Collier and the Origins of Indian Policy Reform* (Albuquerque: University of New Mexico Press, 1983); Kenneth R. Philp, *John Collier's Crusade for Indian reform, 1920–1954* (Tucson: University of Arizona Press, 1977).

22. Vine Deloria, Jr, and Clifford M. Lytle, *The Nations Within: The Past and Future of American Indian Sovereignty* (New York: Pantheon Books Press, 1984).

23. Donald L. Fixico, *Termination and Relocation: Federal Indian Policy, 1945–1960*, (Albuquerque: University of New Mexico Press, 1986).

24. T. S. Lyman, *A History of Indian Policy* (Washington, DC: US Government Printing Office, 1973).

25. United States, American Indian Policy Review Commission, *American Indian Policy Review Commission final report submitted to Congress May 17, 1977* (Washington: US GPO, 1977).

26. John R. Wunder, *Native American Sovereignty* (New York: Garland Press, 1996).

27. Council of Economic Advisers for the President's Initiative on Race. *Changing America: Indicators of Social and Economic Well-Being by Race and Hispanic Origin* (Washington, DC: US Government Printing Office, 1998), p. 10. See the analysis of multiracial census data from the 2000 US Census at www.censusscope.org/us/chart-multi.html

28. W. C. Canby, *American Indian Law In a Nutshell* (St. Paul, Minnesota: West Group Press, 1998); Felix S. Cohen, *Handbook of Federal American Indian Law* (Washington, DC: US Government Printing Service, 1983).

29. Melissa Meyer, 'American Indian blood quantum requirements: blood is thicker than family,' in Valerie J. Matsumoto and Blake Allmendinger (eds), *Over the Edge: Remapping the American West* (Berkeley: University of California Press, 1999), pp. 231–49.

30. Stephen L. Pevar, *The Rights of Indians and Tribes*, 3rd edn (Carbondale and Edwardsville: Southern Illinois University Press, 2002); Wilkins, *American Indian Sovereignty*; Canby, *American Indian Law*.

31. *Babbitt, Secretary of Interior, et al., v. Youpee, et al., 519 U.S. 234* (1997), Certiorari to the US Court of Appeals for the Ninth Circuit, no. 95–1595.

32. Frank Pommersheim, *Braid of Feathers: American Indian Law and Contemporary Tribal Life* (Berkeley: University of California Press, 1995); Nell Jessup Newton,

'Tribal court praxis: one year in the life of twenty indian tribal courts,' 22 Am. Indian L. Rev. (1998), 285–354.

33. Jerry Muskrat, 'The Indian Bill of Rights and the constitutional status of tribal governments,' 82 Harv. L. Rev. 1343, 425–55 (1969).

34. Canby, *American Indian Law*; Perar, *The Rights of Indians*; J. V. White, *Taxing Those They Found Here: An Examination of the Tax Exempt Status of the American Indian* (Washington: Washington Institute for the Development of Indian Law, 1972).

35. Cohen, Handbook of Federal American Indian Law, pp. 786–8.

36. W. Dale Mason, *Indian Gaming: Tribal Sovereignty and American Politics* (Norman: University of Oklahoma Press, 2000).

37. L. Burton, *American Indian Water Rights and the Limitation of the Law* (Lawrence: University of Kansas Press, 1991).

38. Christopher Vecsey, *Handbook of American Indian Religious Freedom* (New York: Crossroad Press, 1991).

39. *Lyng v. Northwest Indian Cemetery Protective Association, 485 US 439 (1988)*.

40. *Employment Division v. Smith, 485 US 660 (1988)*.

41. P. L. 103–344 (6 October 1994), An Act to Amend the American Indian Religious Freedom Act to Provide for the Traditional Use of Peyote by Indians for Religious Purposes.

42. *Mending the Circle: A Native American Repatriation Guide* (New York: Native American Ritual Object Repatriation Foundation, 1996); Rennard Strickland, 'Implementing the national policy of understanding, preserving, and safeguarding the heritage of Indian peoples, sacred objects, and cultural patrimony,' *Arizona State Law Journal*, 24 (Spring, 1992), pp. 175–91; Jack F. Trope and Walter R. Echo-Hawk, 'The Native American Graves Protection and Repatriation Act: background and legislative history,' *Arizona State Law Journal*, vol. 24, no. 1 (Spring 1992), 35–77.

43. *Mississippi Choctaw Indian Band v. Holyfield, 490 US 30 (1989)*.

CHAPTER 5

Language

The fourth premise of Native American/American Indian Studies is that language is key to understanding Native world views. Accordingly most programs teach one or more native language.

Language is a way of categorizing experience, and the study of categories gives insight into the way that people give structure to the world. The study of language provides an epistemological tool for the understanding of culture. In the Navajo pantheon of deities, for example, two of the great creative forces are *sahnagahi*, Thought Boy, and *bi' ke hozho*, Speech Girl.[1] Every outer physical form has an inner, animating form. Thought is the inner form that animates speech. Speech is manifest as breath, which is in turn a manifestation of wind. Wind is the breath of the universe, and it is the force that gives expression to human thought in speech. The small dust devils that move across the southwestern landscape are thus an aspect of spiritual power that is also expressed in human breath. The spiritual power of wind lies in its seemingly random and capricious nature, its wilfulness. Language is breath that is given form by thought. Speaking is the uniquely creative aspect of human spirituality. Prayer, in the form of ritual chants, has the power to evoke desired responses from spiritual forces.[2]

EPISTEMOLOGICAL ASPECTS OF NATIVE LANGUAGES

There are a number of distinctive aspects of native languages that demonstrate their value as epistemological tools. These generalizations do not imply a uniformity of structure in all Native languages but, rather, patterns

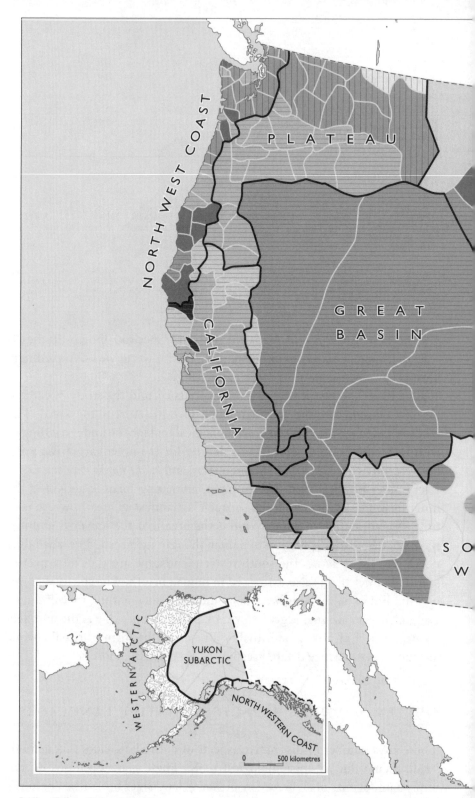

P L A T E A U

NORTH WEST COAST

CALIFORNIA

G R E A T
B A S I N

S O
W

YUKON
SUBARCTIC

WESTERN ARCTIC

NORTH WESTERN COAST

0   500 kilometres

Indian Tribes, Cultures and Languages

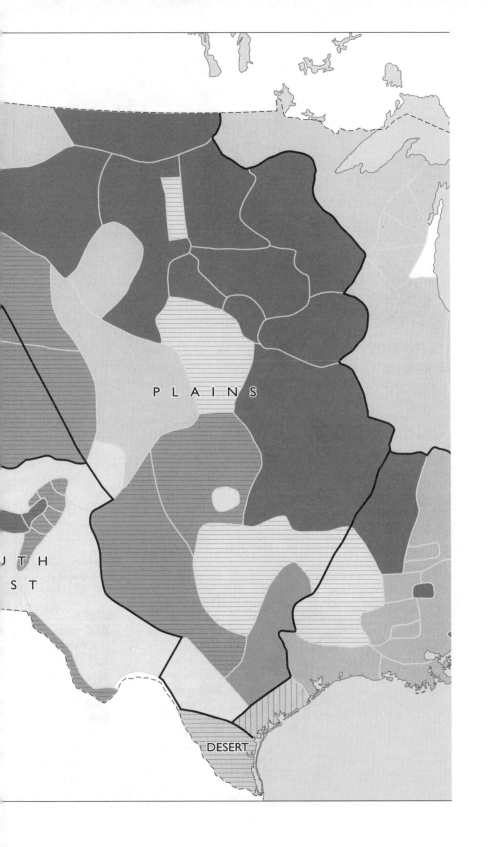

PLAINS

SOUTH
WEST

DESERT

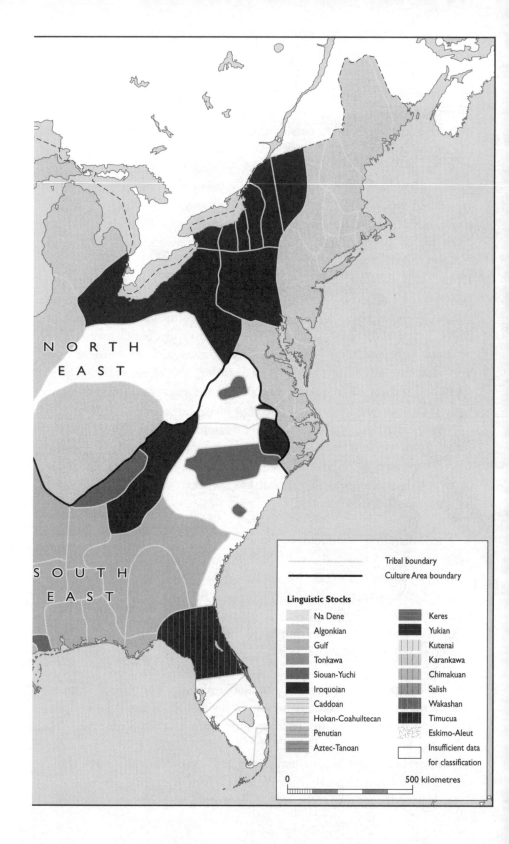

N O R T H
E A S T

S O U T H
E A S T

Tribal boundary

Culture Area boundary

Linguistic Stocks

Na Dene

Algonkian

Gulf

Tonkawa

Siouan-Yuchi

Iroquoian

Caddoan

Hokan-Coahuiltecan

Penutian

Aztec-Tanoan

Keres

Yukian

Kutenai

Karankawa

Chimakuan

Salish

Wakashan

Timucua

Eskimo-Aleut

Insufficient data
for classification

0   500 kilometres

that occur more frequently in Native American languages in other parts of the world.

Native languages distinguish between animate and inanimate nouns (recall the story of Hallowell's conversation with the Ojibwe man about rocks being alive). They also distinguish between objects defined as possessions, such as body parts and relatives, and things like tools or weapons that are owned incidentally. They generally express a sense of place – within, above, beside, and so on – by suffixes to or elements after nouns. They are often highly polysynthetic, that is, they combine elements into single complex words rather than using a number of discrete words to express an action. It is difficult to say, then, that there is a close correspondence between the English noun and the idea of discrete objects in Native language.[3] Thus the Hupa language in California has the word *te-s-e-ya-te*, literally, 'here and there in space in-progress-I-go-future' which means 'I will be going here and there.' As Joel Scherzer puts it, Native world views 'included fine attention to details of position, direction, motion, form, shape and texture, all frequently encoded in and expressed through highly wrought words imaginative and poetic in form.'[4]

Native languages make critical distinctions between knowledge that comes from personal experience and that which comes from hearsay, whereas speakers of English are quite comfortable with making statements of accepted knowledge – 'there are atoms,' or 'there are fifty Eskimo words for snow.' As Kilpatrick notes:

> The Indian finds it difficult to put any reliance in a people who, without a qualm of conscience, have the brassbound effrontery to make a statement such as 'Joe paid his debt.' Does the speaker actually know that Joe came through, or is he reporting hearsay? Cherokee verbs make a prayerful distinction between what the speaker knows to be true from having witnessed an act, and what is merely reputed to be true.[5]

This distinction is a critical epistemological one. The Greek historian Herodotus made this same distinction in his history of the Peloponnesian Wars, and he sought his information only from first-hand observers. His point has largely lost its applicability in contemporary historical studies. Now it serves, for instance, to distinguish native traditions about how things came to be the way they are from Western senses of history.

In Native languages, verbs, as action words, are more important than nouns because of their attention to such factors as the ways in which motion occurs, the physical relationship between speakers, whether action takes place nearby or far away, and the time in which action occurs. As Gary Witherspoon observes, there are 365,200 conjugations of the verb 'to go' in the Navajo language.[6]

Language is a form of categorizing knowledge, and categories are epistemological tools. In the field of anthropology, studies of native systems of classification have been designated as ethnoscience. They are based on linguistic analysis, which as William Sturtevant says, 'provides some insight into the cognitive structures of a world view.'[7]

Association can be the basis for classification. The Thompson River Indians in Canada, for instance, named the wood betony (*Pedicularis bracteosa*) *skikens a sha'ket*, meaning 'companion of willow weed,' because they always found it with the willow.[8] The Apaches, who speak an Athabascan language, categorize objects according to size, shape and texture, and verb forms depend on the nature of the objects upon which they work. For instance, one verb form is used for objects which are two-thirds longer than they are wide, while another form is used if the ratio is less.[9] The Wintun put turtles, automobiles, and overturned bowls in the same category.[10] The Navajo language has twenty-one categories of objects, which are based on similarity of form. Long, hard objects comprise one category; soft goods another; long flexible objects another, thus, snakes and lightning are both in this latter same category.[11]

Ethnoscience in its strictest anthropological sense has focused on eliciting information from native informants and discovering the native principles that determine the kind of congruence that must be present to constitute a category. Such a study of the Ojibwa showed that they had a higher respect for spiritual beings in their world than they did for animals, based on the ability of spirits to control animals.[12]

The Lakota world comprised two categories of living beings – the two-leggeds (birds, bears, and human beings) and the four-leggeds (all beings that go on four legs). The story of the great race that created the Black Hills in south Dakota explains the cultural significance of those categories. The buffalo was leading the four-leggeds to victory when the magpie, which had lighted on his back unbeknownst to him, calmly flew up and over the finish line just as the buffalo reached it. The two-leggeds thus won the race and that meant that humans could eat the four-leggeds, but that they also had a special, respectful and reciprocal relationship with them. The four-leggeds must give themselves to be eaten.

The commonly accepted idea that Eskimos (Inuit, Yupik, Nunamiut, and so on) have fifty names for snow indicates both how little knowledge most Americans have about the complexities of Native cultures and languages and the way in which Native languages express their cultural priorities. Snow may be light and fluffy, or heavy and wet, or icy. It may be blowing, or it may be flattened on the surface of the ground. All these conditions of snow obviously have an impact on the ability of Native people in the Arctic to travel about. The study of native categories of knowledge provides insight into native cultures.[13] It is an important epistemological tool for understanding Native ways of knowing.

LANGUAGE AS METAPHOR

Native languages are often highly metaphorical in their meanings. Words stand for things, but the correspondence between words and things is extraordinarily complex. Verbs may reflect the ongoing relationships among things, but the names of things themselves reflect varying understandings of the ultimate reality of physical objects. Things stand in relationship with each other in terms of action, but words also exist to name real things that have existence. Words are not simply things. They embody complex concepts that express the relationships between physical and spiritual forces. Consider the statement of a young Santa Clara Pueblo woman who said, 'When I dance, I am the corn.' What she was expressing was her sense of identity with corn.

Metaphor in English is generally considered a figure of speech, but its intellectual power has been emphasized by modern scholars. George Lakoff, for example, gives an extended discussion of the metaphor 'War is hell.'[14] In Native languages, metaphors express a profound intellectual understanding that the human and the physical worlds are intimately related. In Nahuatl, the language of the Aztec empire, for example, the word for white was derived from the word for salt, red from the word for blood, and green from a general word for plants. The Quiche language in Latin America used the words for parts of the human body to express basic concepts of the position of objects in the world – the head for the top, and so on. Mayan languages generally associated parts of the body with other objects, hence the bark of the tree was its skin, a door was a mouth.[15] The Apache use an elaborate metaphorical set of terms for body parts to refer to parts of an automobile.[16]

In an epistemological sense, we learn by analogy, that is, by comparing unfamiliar elements to familiar ones and thus being able to fit them into existing categories. Natives on the northwest coast, for instance, found that metal bells could replace deer hoofs on dance aprons because of the similarity of sounds between the clinking of the hoofs and of the bells.[17] Metaphors, on the other hand, assert an identity between two dissimilar objects. Metaphors do not compare the unknown to the known. Rather, they make associations that make sense within accepted intellectual constructs in a society. In a contemporary Yuchi ceremony in Oklahoma, shotguns are fired to replicate the sound of thunder as an essential part of ceremonial songs.[18] Although the sound of the gun may have suggested the sound of thunder upon first experience, the sound is the thunder in the song.

The power of metaphor is evident in the Cherokee story of Selu, the corn mother, related in Chapter 3. Read as a literal narrative, it tells the story of two boys who kill their mother and discover corn growing where her blood had touched the ground. Read as metaphor, however, it explains the deep connection between human fertility and the fertility of the earth, the profound connection between seasonal cycles, agricultural cycles, and the cycles of birth and death in human life.

Studies of native cultures by Western scholars have, by the very nature of the investigators' intellectual preconceptions, proceeded by analogy – comparing the knowledge of native people to their own knowledge. Metaphor, however, is a culturally based way of knowing. By asserting identity between the corn and her own personal identity, the young woman who is the corn expresses the relationship between the physical, material world and the spiritual, ceremonial world of Santa Clara Pueblo.

This power of metaphor is evident in the multiple meanings that words have in native languages. The Iroquoian term for spiritual power, *orenda*, is also the word meaning 'to pray.' The act of praying is thus the same as using one power to bring about a result. By examining the multiple meanings of single words, one can explore the metaphorical nature of Native languages. An excellent example of this kind of study is Leanne Hinton's explication of a Wintu (Northern California) doctoring song. Grace McKibben, a Wintu woman, learned the song from her uncle. The essence of the song, which is highly repetitious, is about white prostitutes going along the street swaying on their high heels. To McKibben, the song presented a humorous image of heavily made-up women walking precariously down the street. Hinton's linguistic analysis of the song, however, points out that the Wintu word for prostitute is related to the word for 'suckerfish,' a powerful spirit often controlled by doctors. The relationship may have to do with the physical similarity of the bulging eyes and large lips of the fish with the eye make-up and lipstick of the prostitute. Hinton cites two Wintu traditions that associate the suckerfish with curing power. She concludes that

> Perhaps Buckskin Bob was implying that the white presence was a kind of spirit, a disease; or perhaps he was making a metaphor for the change the white man brought to shamanism and to Wintu culture as a whole. Or perhaps it was more subtle and involved more than that. In any case, it is clear that Bob Brown [the doctor] was taking modern images and interweaving them with traditional medical concerns through the traditional shamanistic means of making a play on words.[19]

THE SOCIAL IMPLICATIONS OF LANGUAGE

Because Native languages were not written, they have much more immediate connotations for social behavior. Walter Ong has explored the dimensions of purely oral language by pointing out that hearing is more real or existential than the other senses, and that it situates people in the middle of actuality and simultaneity because sound can come from all directions at once, whereas vision puts people in front of things and creates linearity. He maintains that visual orientations and aural orientations create different kinds of personality structures and that 'A world of sounds thus tends to grow into a world of voices and of persons, those most unpredictable of all creatures.'[20] A world of pure orality demands constant social interaction. Perhaps this fact explains the concern of native languages with action and proximity.

Although knowledge was conveyed through oral communication, certain kinds of knowledge could be recorded in structures or objects that served as mnemonic devices. Medicine wheels, for instance, are permanent markers of solstice points on the horizon. Incised birchbark scrolls helped Midewiwin practitioners among the Ojibwa to remember the sequence of the origin stories that were recited during their ceremonies. Wampum belts had their meanings spoken into them and as physical objects carried the essence of agreements. The famous William Penn wampum belt signifies the agreement that the Iroquois tribes made with early English settlers. Winter counts, the pictorial records of Plains tribes, were accounts of unique events in tribal experience.

The oral traditions of Native cultures are the major repositories of tribal knowledge and values. Storytelling is an excellent example of the power of spoken language. In Keith Basso's seminal article 'Stalking with Stories,' a young woman who had recently returned from boarding school attended a ceremony with her hair in pink plastic rollers. Although her appearance was inappropriate for the ceremony, she was not scolded publicly. Subsequently, however, she visited her grandmother, who for no immediately discernible reason suddenly told a story of an Apache who killed a white man's cow and was subsequently apprehended, but then released, by another Apache man who was serving as a policeman for the United States Indian agent. The incident occurred at a place named Ndee Dah Naaziné (Men Stand Above Here and There). The story meant that the Apache policeman was acting too much like a white man in arresting his fellow tribesman. When the girl heard it, she knew it was in reference to her behavior at the ceremony, which was attributed to her being too much influenced by the white school. Whenever she passed the place called Ndee Dah Naaziné, she was reminded of her behavior. The telling of a story thus associates the name of a place with human activities that took place at some time in the past. In some cases, these activities contravened tribal values and led to negative consequences. Stories about places and the places themselves thus remind people of what constitutes appropriate behavior.[21]

THE CULTURAL IMPLICATIONS OF LANGUAGE LOSS

There were approximately 500 distinct languages in North America at the time of European contact. Each was a unique way of expressing the range of human relationships to the physical and spiritual worlds, and to other humans. Shirley Silver and Wick Miller reported that in 1960 there were approximately 175 languages north of Mexico, of which 136 had less than 2,000 speakers, and thirty-four had no more than ten speakers.[22] According to Yves Goddard, in the early twenty-first century, about half of those languages have disappeared and many of the rest are in danger of dying with the generation of elders who are the last speakers.[23]

The processes leading to language loss must be laid directly on the policy of the United States government to assimilate American Indians into American society. The mechanism of that policy was, of course, the federal or mission boarding school. The Civilization Act of 1819 promised financial support to 'benevolent associations' that would undertake to teach

Indians to read and write (presumably in English). The benevolent associations were generally Christian missionary organizations whose primary purpose was to convert Indians to Christianity. The problem of language lay at the heart of their efforts.

The missionaries of the American Board of Commissioners for Foreign Missions who established their first station in the Choctaw Nation in 1818 lamented that there were no words in Choctaw for Christian concepts such as sin, guilt, and redemption, and although some of the Choctaws had 'some confused notion of a great Being above', they did not know 'what his character is, or what he requires them to do.' Indeed, many had 'not the least idea of a superior being.'[24] Choctaws believed that their souls (the *shilombish*, or shadow, and the *shilup*, or ghost) persisted after death, but there was no consensus as to what happened to them.

The 'confused notion of a great Being above' stemmed from the fact that the Choctaws had several words for spiritual power – *Nanapesa*, which bilingual Choctaws translated as 'director' or 'judge;' *Ishtahullo-chito*, a term applied 'to whatever excites surprise, and also to anything which they conceive to possess some occult or superior power;' *Hushtahli*, from *Hashi*, 'sun,' and *tahli*, 'to complete an action;' and *Aba Pi^{n}ki*, 'Our Father,' evidently a borrowing from English. The term Hushtahli was probably the closest to the Christian concept because the Sun was the primary physical manifestation of spiritual power for the Choctaws. Fire was the sun's earthly representation, and the Choctaw burial custom of exposing the bodies of the dead on platforms to decay was a way of returning the essence of the individual to the power of the sun.[25]

Cyrus Byington, one of the American Board Missionaries, translated Christian concepts into the Choctaw language, but an examination of his glosses of words in his dictionary of Choctaw reveals the differing understandings that native Choctaw speakers had.[26] His gloss of 'sin' includes the following words: *aiashachi, aiashachika, aiyoshoba, ashachi, na yoshobanan aiashacheka, nan ashacheka, nan ashachi, and yoshoba*. The first word, *aiashachi*, he glosses first as a transitive verb meaning 'to err at; to make a mistake at, or by means of; to sin about, or at,; to overlook.' *Aiashachika* he glosses as a noun meaning 'a sin; a mistake.' *Aiyoshoba* is a noun meaning 'error, wandering; sin; place of sin.' In this rendering, the root *yoshoba* is glossed as 'lost; out of the way, gone astray; sinful, evil, wicked, guilty, ill; immoral; iniquitous; reprobate; vicious, wanton' (p. 375). To a contemporary Christian Choctaw speaker, the primary meaning of *yoshoba* is wandering in the wilderness, as wild animals do (the connection to *nashoba*, wolf, indicates the primacy of this meaning). The Choctaw speaker hearing Byington preach about sin would understand it either as a form of mistake or losing one's way in the woods. Such meanings convey by extension some aspects of sin in Christianity but they certainly do not connote the depths of human depravity that sin represented in the strongly Calvinist tradition of the Presbyterian Church.

Where Presbyterian theology stressed man's total subjection to the will of God, the Choctaw language emphasized the concepts of *kostini*, to be in control of things, and *haksi*, to be out of control. These glosses by a contemporary Choctaw speaker contrast rather markedly with Byington's definition of *kostini* as 'sense; understanding; chastity; mansuetude; probity, purity, reform; sanity; sobriety' (p. 238), and *haksi* as 'deaf, drunk; . . . cunning; wicked; vile . . .' (p. 132). To the Choctaws, human beings had the power to control their own lives, and loss of control through improper behavior (hence the gloss of 'drunkenness') was a shameful state. The physical manifestation of power in Choctaw beliefs was the Sun, but it is unlikely that the missionaries would have accepted the Sun as the equivalent of the God whose power they were trying to teach to the Choctaws.[27]

This one example gives some idea of the profound intellectual gulf that separated Choctaw speakers from the missionaries, and although Cyrus Byington learned Choctaw sufficiently to preach with some proficiency in the language, we can only wonder at what his audiences were able to make of his words. The American Board of Commissioners initially supported the education of children in their native languages, the better to prepare them to receive Christian doctrine, but by the 1820s it had recognized the difficulties of the missionaries' mastering those languages sufficiently to do their work, and determined that education in its schools should be in English.

The suppression of Native languages in boarding schools did not lead students to lose their own languages; it often engendered resistance. Frances LaFlesche's account of his experience in a boarding school shows both the policy to suppress language and, at the same time, the students' strategies to thwart that policy. It also shows how students actually learned other native languages from their classmates in covert situations.[28]

THE PROBLEM OF TRANSLATION

The difficulties of translation are illustrated both in the Choctaw example above and in John Heckwelder's attempt to learn the Delaware language.

Following his understanding of European noun-based languages, he pointed at things to elicit a name from the Natives, but he was puzzled when the response was the same no matter what he pointed at. As he began to learn the language, he finally learned that the word with which the Delaware responded to his pointing at objects was the word for forefinger.[29]

The problem of translation has existed from the first interactions of Indian tribes with each other and from when they first encountered Europeans. It derives from all of the above mentioned aspects of Native languages. Native understanding of Christian concepts complicated the process of conversion of Native people to Christianity. The supposed understanding achieved in treaties between Native people and representatives of foreign governments was often questionable. Indeed, the legal principle that treaties must be interpreted in favor of Indians where that interpretation is ambiguous has been enunciated in court decisions since the original Marshall decisions in the 1830s.

The work of translation demands not only knowledge of vocabulary, grammar and syntax, but it demands understanding of cultural nuances, and, when languages being translated do not have written text, it demands attention to setting, tone of voice, gestures, and body language.[30] In storytelling situations, where much of cultural understanding is transmitted, it is not enough to translate only the words. Scholars have recognized this fact. Dennis Tedlock's translation of Zuni oral traditions employed typography to indicate aspects of storytelling such as loudness or softness of speech and emphasis in words. Brenda Farnell used videotape, and analyzed gestures and positionality as essential elements of storytelling.[31]

THE POLITICAL IMPLICATIONS OF LANGUAGE

The federal government policy of assimilating Native people into American society explicitly acknowledged the power of language as a cultural marker by forbidding students from speaking their native languages. Boarding schools both suppressed Native languages and, because they facilitated intermarriage of students from different tribes, created situations in which English became the *lingua franca* of multilingual households. Contemporary Indian communities have retained the use of their languages to a greater or lesser degree. In communities that are losing their languages, speakers are generally in their sixties, or older. People in their forties may understand some of the spoken language, but generally cannot speak it themselves. In relatively few communities are native languages spoken in homes so that children can learn them. Navajo is still the community language in remote parts of the reservation; Lakota is still heard in communities in North and South Dakota; the Mississippi Choctaw communities still use the language on a regular basis. Even in these tribes, however, English is becoming the commonly accepted *lingua franca*, and indeed, the Mississippi Choctaw tribal government sponsors a summer immersion language camp to help children gain fluency in Choctaw.[32] In the past Indian parents often spoke their language to each other to discuss things about which they did not wish their children to know. Native communities have increasingly realized the implications of the loss of language to their unique identities. Various pieces of federal legislation have reversed policies to suppress native languages (see the Native American Languages Acts (P.L. 101–477, 1990 and P.L. 102–524, 1992), although 'English only' initiatives appear regularly at the state level. Such initiatives are implicit acknowledgements of the political nature of language.

Language has both cultural and political importance in contemporary Native societies. Many communities have mounted language revitalization programs, utilizing the memories of surviving speakers and word lists, dictionaries and rudimentary grammars often written by missionaries who tried to master native languages in order to convert American Indians to Christianity, and by nineteenth-century ethnologists who recognized the significance of language as a way of gaining insights into cultural values, and so sought to preserve languages in a permanent, written form.[33] The federal government has provided funding for efforts to preserve Native languages through the Administration for Native Americans in the Health and Human Services Department, which had a budget of $3.7 million in FY 2002 to support language development proposals. Universities have taken advantage of linguistic scholarship and the expertise of speakers of Native languages to develop courses. For instance, the University of Arizona offers courses in Navajo and Hopi, the University of Alaska at Fairbanks offers courses in Gwich'in (an Athabascan language) and Yu'pik and Inupiaq (Eskimo languages). The University of Oklahoma offers Creek, Choctaw, Cherokee, and Kiowa.[34]

The University of Arizona offers another resource for strengthening community-based language retention efforts. The American Indian Language Development Institute, founded in 1978, offers intensive four-week summer training programs aimed at training speakers of Native languages in the basic principles of linguistics, research, and bicultural curriculum development that they can use in schools and community-based programs in their communities.

Community-based programs, many funded through Administration for Native Americans grants, include such variations as master/apprentice programs (see the journal *News from Native California*, published by Malcolm Margolin in Berkeley, California), online real-time instruction in Choctaw offered through the Choctaw Nation in Oklahoma, summer language immersion camps for children offered by the Mississippi Band of Choctaw Indians, and evening classes for adult learners conducted through the Comanche tribe of Oklahoma. Many community programs come and go with vagaries of funding and availability of teachers. The significance of such programs, however, is that Native people see language retention as an issue for cultural survival, and more tools are becoming available to assist people who want to start such programs.[35]

Languages remain, however, a political issue for Native American Studies programs. Dialectical differences inherent in spoken language inspire debate over who is speaking correctly. Differences in men's and women's speech complicate the issue of teaching a language as a standard form of speech. Some community members of the Absentee Shawnee Tribe of Oklahoma, for instance, feel that language, as an inherent cultural characteristic, should not be taught to anyone other than tribal members.

CONCLUSION

Language provides the deepest insights into ways in which Native people function within their physical and cultural environments. It is a critical epistemological tool for understanding cultural differences. Native languages stress the importance of actions, relationships, attention to fine distinctions in form and texture of objects. The very act of speaking is recognized as a creative force in the world. Native languages classify the aspects of the world around them with attention to those details and how beings interact with one another. They make crucial distinctions between experiential knowledge and what is learned from others. In all these ways they express the very essence of human knowledge.

The suppression of Indian languages was for decades a part of governmental policy to assimilate Indians into American society. Federal policymakers recognized that language is an essential aspect of cultural identity. Christian missionaries learned and recorded Native languages primarily so they could then educate Native children in English. It is ironic that knowledge of Native languages in communities in Oklahoma often persists for those who do not speak the languages in the form of Christian hymns sung in those languages, for example 'Amazing Grace' sung in Cherokee is a standard part of the repertoire of the Cherokee Nation Children's Choir. Choctaws and Kiowas who speak little of their language can also sing a number of hymns.

The preservation and revitalization of Indian languages becomes an act of asserting cultural identity and reclaiming a heritage that was often forcibly taken from them. The passage of federal and in some cases state legislation (Oklahoma 1017) allowing the teaching of Native languages has become important for tribal and cultural sovereignty. Although not widely utilized, these legislative actions provide an entrée in state school districts for Native language instruction.

The crucial question in Native American Studies programs is, what can the teaching of Native languages accomplish for Native communities? Language is a key marker of cultural identity, and students, native and non-native, can achieve a certain level of competence in speaking and writing native languages, but the question remains – to whom can they speak, and who will read what they write? For those doing research in communities, where the business and social life is carried on in English, learning the Native language may not be a necessity for gathering information, but it is a sign that an individual is willing to try to gain some degree of solidarity with community members and that s/he realizes the significance of cultural nuances. The study of Native language is one of the most important, and one of the most contentious, issues for any Native American Studies program. It cuts to the heart of Indian identity, federal policy, and contemporary efforts to recover language as a marker of cultural identity.

NOTES

1. Gary Witherspoon, *Language and Art in the Navajo Universe* (Ann Arbor: University of Michigan Press, 1977).
2. Gladys A. Reichard, *Prayer: the Compulsive Word* (New York: J. J. Augustin, 1944).
3. Marianne Minthun, 'Overview of general characteristics,' in *Handbook of North American Indians*, vol. 17, *Language* (Washington, DC: Smithsonian Institution, 1996), pp. 137–57.
4. Joel Scherzer, 'À richness of voices,' in Alvin Josephy (ed.), *America in 1492* (New York: Alfred A. Knopf, 1992), pp. 253–5.

5. Jack Kilpatrick, 'Verbs are king on Panther Hill,' *Southwest Review* (Autumn 1961), 373.

6. Witherspoon, *Language and Art*, p. 48.

7. William C. Sturtevant, 'Studies in ethnoscience,' in J. P. Spradley (ed.), *Culture and Cognition: Rules, Maps, and Plans* (San Francisco: Chandler, 1972), pp. 129–67, quoting p. 130).

8. James Teit, *Ethnobotany of the Thompson Indians of British Columbia, based on Field Notes by James A. Teit*, ed. Elsie Viault Steedman, *Forty-Fifth Annual Report of the Bureau of American ethnology 1927–28* (Washington, DC: Smithsonian Institution, 1930), pp. 450–1, 468, 500.

9. Keith H. Basso, *Western Apache Language and Culture: Essays in Linguistic Anthropology* (Tucson: University of Arizona Press, 1990), pp. 15–24.

10. Dorothy Lee, *Freedom and Culture* (Englewood Cliffs, NJ: Prentice-Hall Publishers, 1959).

11. Witherspoon, *Language and Art*, p. 48.

12. Mary B. Black, 'Ojibwa power belief system,' in Raymond D. Fogelson and Richard N. Adams (eds), *The Anthropology of Power: Ethnographic Studies from Asia, Oceania, and the New World* (New York: Academic Press, 1977).

13. Brent Berlin, Dennis Breedlove, and Peter H. Raven, *Principles of Tzeltal Plant Classification: An Introduction to the Botanical Ethnography of a Mayan-Speaking People of Highland Chiapas* (New York: Academic Press, 1974), p. xv.

14. George Lakoff and Mark Johnson, *Metaphors We Live By* (Chicago: University of Chicago Press 1980).

15. Sherzer, 'A richness of voices,' pp. 256–7.

16. Basso, *Western Apache Language*, pp. 20–1.

17. H. G. Barnett, 'Invention and cultural change,' *American Anthropologist*, XLIV (January–March, 1942), 23–6.

18. Gary White Deer, 'Pretty Shellshaker,' in Dayna Bowker Lee (ed.), *Remaining Ourselves: Music and Tribal Memory* (Oklahoma City: State Arts Council of Oklahoma, 1995), pp. 11–14.

19. Leanne Hinton and Alice Shepherd, 'Layers of meaning in a Wintu doctor song,' *The Life of Language: Papers in Linguistics in Honor of William Bright*, ed. Jane H. Hill, P. J. Mistry, Lyle Campbell (Berlin, New York: Mouton de Gruyter, 1998), p. 279.

20. Walter J. Ong, *The Presence of the Word; Some Prolegomena for Cultural and Religious History* (New Haven: Yale University Press, 1967), pp. 117, 128, 131.

21. Keith Basso, 'Stalking with stories,' in *Wisdom Sits in Places: Landscape and Language Among the Western Apache* (Albuquerque: University of New Mexico Press, 1996), pp. 54–7.

22. Shirley Silver and Wick R. Miller, *American Indian Languages: Cultural and Social Contexts* (Tucson: University of Arizona Press, 1997), p. 8.

23. Ives Goddard, 'Introduction,' to *Handbook of North American Indians*, vol. 17, *Languages* (Washington, DC: Smithsonian Institution, 1996), p. 3.

24. Journal of Mayhew Mission, 17 January 1822, American Board of Commissioners for Foreign Missions Papers, series 18.1.3, vol. 1, folder 79, Houghton Library, Harvard University.

25. John R. Swanton, *Source Material for the Social and Ceremonial Life of the Choctaw Indians*, Bureau of American Ethnology Bulletin, no. 103 (Washington, DC: Government Printing Office, 1931), p. 216.

26. Cyrus Byington, *A Dictionary of the Choctaw Language*, ed. J. R. Swanton, and H. S. Halbert, The Smithsonian Institution, Bureau of American Ethnography, Bulletin 46 (Washington, DC: Government Printing Office, 1915).

27. Swanton, *Source Material*, p. 195.

28. Francis La Flesche, *The Middle Five: Indian Schoolboys of the Omaha Tribe* (Madison: University of Wisconsin Press, 1963).

29. John Gottlieb Ernestus Heckwelder, *An Account of the History, Manners, and Customs, of the Indian Nations, who once Inhabited Pennsylvania and the Neighbouring States* (Philadelphia: A. Small, 1819).

30. Dell H. Hymes, *'In vain I tried to tell you': Essays in Native American Ethnopoetics* (Philadelphia: University of Pennsylvania Press, 1981); Dennis Tedlock, *The Spoken Word and the Work of Interpretation* (Philadelphia: University of Pennsylvania Press, 1983).

31. Dennis Tedlock, *Finding the Center; Narrative Poetry of the Zuñi Indians*, trans. Dennis Tedlock, from performances in the Zuñi by Andrew Peynetsa and Walter Sanchez (New York: Dial Press, 1972); Brenda M. Farnell, *Do You See What I Mean?: Plains Indian Sign Talk and the Embodiment of Action* (Austin: University of Texas Press, 1995).

32. See the *Choctaw Community New*, published by the Mississippi Band of Choctaw Indians, summer, 2002, *passim*.

33. Roger Williams, *A key into the language of America, or, An help to the language of the natives in that part of America, Called New-England: together, with briefe observations of the customes, manners and worships, &c. of the aforesaid natives, in peace and warre, in life and death: on all which are added spirituall observations, generall and particular by the authour, of chiefe and speciall use (upon all occasions,) to all the English inhabiting those parts; yet pleasant and profitable to the view of all men* (London: printed by Gregory Dexter, 1643); Franz Boas, *Introduction to Handbook of American Indian Languages*, ed. Preston Holder (Lincoln: University of Nebraska Press, 1966); John Wesley Powell, *Linguistic Stocks of American Indians North of Mexico*; compiled under the direction of Henry Garnett, United States, Bureau of American Ethnology, Seventh Annual Report pl. 1 (Washington, DC: Bureau of American Ethnology, 1903).

34. See the online publication 'A Guide to Native American Studies Programs in the United States and Canada,' ed. Robert M. Nelson for the Association for the Study of American Indian Literature. (http://oncampus.richmond.edu/faculty/ASAIL/guide/guide1.html)

35. Leanne Hinton and Ken Hale, *The Green Book of Language Revitalization in Practice* (San Diego: Academic Press, 2001).

CHAPTER 6

Indian Aesthetics: Literature

As a field of study, Indian literature may be defined as literature by Indians about Indians.[1] This is a provisional guideline rather than a hard and fast rule, since many Indian writers, being Americans who spend much of their time among non-Indians, write books that include both Indian and non-Indian characters. For the most part, however (like other American ethnic writers – Jews, Blacks, Asians, for instance) Indians tend primarily to write about their own ethnic group.

Before contact with whites, Indians in North America had a strong literary tradition, which was for the most part oral.[2] The principal forms were the tale and song. The tale was primarily narrative, but to an extent the narrator's mimicry of characters resembled drama. Songs were primarily musical rather than literary, but their lyrics made them a species of lyric poetry as well. The traditions of tales and songs remain strong among the tribes, and have influenced Indian literature in English, which is the principal focus of this chapter.

Indians have been writing in English since 1768 when Samson Occom, a Mohegan, composed an autobiographical essay. Occom's later work, 'Sermon Preached at the Execution of Moses Paul, an Indian' (1772), was, according to intellectual historian Jace Weaver (Cherokee), 'an early best-seller' in New England. The first novel by an Indian writer is Cherokee journalist Rollin Ridge's *The Life and Adventures of Joaquin Murieta, the Celebrated California Bandit*, published in 1854. Ridge, a fugitive from Oklahoma for a political murder of a fellow Cherokee, gives a highly sympathetic and melodramatic portrayal of Murieta as a 'Mexican-American Robin Hood,' to quote Weaver.

Until 1968 Indian writers produced only a handful of novels, the best of which were *Sundown* (1934) by John Joseph Matthews (Osage), and *The Surrounded* (1936) by D'Arcy McNickle (Cree/Metis, enrolled Salish).[3] The books could not show more different pictures of Indian life in the first half of the twentieth century. *Sundown* is the story of an Osage man, Chal Windzer, who enrolls at the University of Oklahoma. He plays football and joins a fraternity. His problems concern defining himself and finding an identity, and unable to do this to his satisfaction at the University, he drops out and joins the Army. The novel ends on an ambiguous note, with Chal stating his purpose to attend law school.

Despite his affluent background – the Osages came into substantial wealth through discovery of oil on their lands – Chal's problems are not trivial. Osages found that their wealth did not shield them fully from the severe psychological stresses caused by the assault on their traditional culture. There are mixed-blood Salish with some money in McNickle's *The Surrounded*, but for the most part the disoriented Indians in the book do not have wealth to cushion the shock of the damage to their traditional lifestyle. McNickle employs the bleakest sort of naturalism to depict the destruction of Indian characters who never have a chance in a world they cannot understand.

Before 1968 Indians produced a few works in other genres besides the novel. In the late nineteenth century, Alexander Posey (Creek) wrote highly romantic poetry, along with far more sophisticated political satires that still make interesting reading. Lynn Riggs (Cherokee) wrote several successful plays, the best known of which, *Green Grow the Lilacs* (1930), was the basis for the musical *Oklahoma!*

The year 1968 marks a watershed in Indian intellectual achievement in the United States. The publication of N. Scott Momaday's Pulitzer Prize winning novel *House Made of Dawn* began what has come to be called the 'American Indian renaissance.'[4] Since *House* appeared, Indian writers have published over 200 novels.[5]

Momaday's success inspired a generation of Indian writers, most prominent of whom are James Welch (Blackfeet), Leslie Silko (Laguna), Gerald Vizenor (Chippewa), and Louise Erdrich (Chippewa). A second generation has now appeared, the most successful of whom is Sherman Alexie (Spokane).

Indian writers have influenced each other greatly. Momaday's *House Made of Dawn* is about a soldier who returns home from the Second World War psychologically damaged. Welch's first novel, *Winter in the Blood*

(1974), is about a feckless protagonist who drifts aimlessly in a Montana landscape that Welch depicts as a wasteland, with a conscious reference to T. S. Eliot's use of the Myth of the Holy Grail. Leslie Silko's first novel, *Ceremony* (1977), borrows Momaday's damaged veteran and Welch's wasteland setting, only she uses Laguna myths about the responsibility of the hero for the health of the land instead of the Grail Myth.[6] In order to tell her story she invents a form Momaday calls a 'telling,' which goes far further than Eliot, Hemingway, or Fitzgerald in incorporating the myths into her narrative. Momaday adapts this new form in his next novel, *The Ancient Child* (1989), which culminates with the hero turning into a bear. In Vizenor's first novel, *Darkness in Saint Louis Bearheart* (1978), the hero had turned into a bear. In Louise Erdrich's novel *The Bingo Palace* (1993), one of the heroines turns into a bear.[7]

Although works by Indians reflect particular tribal viewpoints, as well as general American views and values, we may discern certain aspects of a pan-Indian aesthetic. In particular, this manifests itself in a series of inter-related themes, most important of which are the relationship of a tribe to particular lands, connections to tribal traditions and languages, relationships of Indians to nature in general and animals in particular, and assumptions about concepts of time. These concepts are so interwoven that it is difficult to discuss them separately.

We begin with Indians' relationship to the land, but because this is tied up with religion, which is often given expression in stories, we must discuss these things together. Indian writers generally have a very strong sense of place in their novels. Scott Momaday, who began the American Indian renaissance with the virtually simultaneous publication of his novel *House Made of Dawn* and memoir *The Way to Rainy Mountain*, is particularly adept at delivering a powerfully rendered setting. *The Way to Rainy Mountain* takes place in western Oklahoma, where Scott was born. *House Made of Dawn* is set in Jemez, New Mexico, where he grew up. Momaday establishes a pattern in *House* in which he begins a section of the novels by describing the land, then moves to the indigenous fauna, and finally gets to the people who inhabit the place. The section entitled 'July 28' begins:

> The canyon is a ladder to the plain. The valley is pale in the end of
> July when the corn and melons come and age and slowly the fields
> are made ready for the yield, and a faint false air of autumn – an
> illusion still in the land – rises somewhere away in the high north
> country, a vague suspicion of red and yellow on the farthest summits

> . . . There is a kind of life that is peculiar to the land in summer – a
> wariness, a seasonal equation of well-being and awareness. Road
> runners take on the shape of motion itself, urgent and angular . . .
> Higher, among the hills and mesas and sandstone cliffs there are
> foxes and bobcats and mountain lions . . . (pp. 54–6)

Momaday describes other wild animals, mentions domestic animals, and
finally getting to human inhabitants. He starts with the original denizens,
the Anasazi (a Tanoan word for 'Old Ones') before moving to the people
who currently occupy the town of Walatowa, a traditional tribal name for
Jemez Pueblo.

The lyricism and intense feeling of this passage, which in its entirety
stretches three pages, is indicative of the passion Momaday feels for the
country around Jemez. It is true that until Americans became urbanized or
suburbanized, many of them felt a love and sense of belonging to a particular area. As Malcolm Cowley writes in *Exile's Return*:

> Somewhere the turn of a dirt road or the unexpected crest of a hill
> reveals your own childhood, the fields where you once played
> barefoot, the kindly trees, the landscape by which all others are
> measured and condemned.[8]

Cowley, obviously moved himself, continues for over a page in this lyrical
vein describing bottom lands and cornfields. But, the feeling Cowley is
describing is a good deal weaker than the Indian passion for their lands. For
Indians the love of land is rooted in traditional tribal religion, even if they
are also Christian.[9] In his religious manifesto *God is Red*, Vine Deloria
(Sioux) explains that in their religion and philosophy white Americans val-
orize time, whereas Indians give priority to space – that is, land:

> When the domestic ideology is divided according to American
> Indian and Western European immigrant . . . the fundamental
> difference is one of great philosophical importance. American
> Indians hold their lands – places – as having the highest possible
> meaning, and all their statements are made with this reference point
> in mind. Immigrants review the movement of their ancestors across
> the continent as a steady progression of basically good events and
> experiences, thereby placing history – time – in the best possible
> light.[10]

The religious consequence of this philosophical difference is that to Indians the sacred involves a place, 'be it a river, a mountain, a plateau, valley, or other natural feature.'[11] For Euro-Americans the sacred involves an event, for example, the crucifixion, or the original Passover.

Another way to describe the difference between white and Indian attitudes is to state that Indians think in terms belonging to the land, being part of it, whereas whites tend to think in terms of owning it but not being controlled by it. Frank Pommersheim, in his examination of Indian law, *Braid of Feathers*, explains the Indian perspective: 'Land is basic to Indian people; they are part of it and it is part of them; it is their Mother.'[12] In explaining the white viewpoint, Pommersheim quotes Frederick Jackson Turner:

> To *take* possession without being possessed: to take secure hold on the lands beyond and yet hold them at a rigidly maintained spiritual distance. It was never to merge, to mingle, to marry. To do so was to become an apostate from Christian history and so be kept in an eternal wilderness.[13]

A repeated theme in the fiction of Indian writers is that the health of the land and the health of its people are intrinsically related. In *House Made of Dawn*, the protagonist Abel, suffers from what we would call today post-traumatic stress syndrome. He has returned from the Second World War badly scarred emotionally. Instinctively he knows that his recovery is tied to regaining a sense of his place in his world, the world of Walatowa and its environs. He somehow intuits that a song may be the key to reforging his link to the land.

> He was alone, and he wanted to make a song out of the colored canyon, the way the women of Torreon made songs upon their looms out of colored yarn, but he had not got the right words together. It would have been a creation song; he would have sung lowly of the first world, of fire and flood, And of the emergence of the dawn from the hills. (p. 57)

Eventually Abel finds the song: a relative, Benally, teaches him the Navajo creation song 'House Made of Dawn.' At the end of the novel Abel sings the song as he runs in a traditional Walatowan rite, a long-distance race for good hunting and harvests. The runners traverse the reservation, bonding with the land in the process. It is clear that Abel is finally on his way to spiritual and physical health.

Like songs, stories are important in the process of restoring a land, or maintaining order there. This theme is central to the work of Leslie Silko (Laguna), another writer who links the health of a character with the state of his tribal lands. In *Ceremony* the protagonist Tayo, a Second World War veteran, has an even more severe case of post-traumatic stress syndrome than Abel. Tayo is severely delusional, and treatments offered by white psychiatrists have not been able to cure him. Tayo served in the Philippines, and his problems stem from seeing his brother killed by a Japanese soldier, and from the rash prayer he made that the incessant rains would stop. His prayer has resulted in a drought on the Laguna reservation. Tayo abandons white medicine for treatment by shamans, the most important being an old Navajo named Betonie who outlines a quest for Tayo, involving the rescue of a herd of spotted cattle from a white man's fenced field, and a battle with witches. With the aid of two mysterious and perhaps divine figures, Mountain Lion and his wife, Abel completes his sacred task, bringing the rain which ends the drought and restores the reservation.

Silko permeates her novel with Pueblo myths, the stories which her people tell to maintain order in their universe. Although they may seem familiar to many American readers for their similarity to the myth of the Holy Grail – the wasteland, the questing hero, the mysterious female helper, the freeing of the waters – the myths are native to Laguna and other Keresan pueblos. It is a common modernist technique to incorporate myth into fiction: Hemingway, Fitzgerald, and Malamud use the Grail Myth, in fact. However, what Silko is doing is different. As Louis Owens (Choctaw) puts it,

> Silko moves far beyond anything imagined by T. S. Eliot when he wrote on the usefulness of mythological structures in literature. Rather than a previously conceived metaphorical framework within which the anarchy and futility of 'real' (as opposed to mythic) existence can be ordered, as often occurs in modernist texts, mythology in *Ceremony* insists upon its actual simultaneity with and interpenetration into the events of the everyday mundane world.[14]

In traditional Indian societies telling sacred stories is a way of maintaining the order of the world, or restoring it if it has been damaged. Before she begins her narrative, Silko tells the reader about the stories s/he will encounter in her tale:

I will tell you something about stories. . .
  They aren't just entertainment.
    Don't be fooled.
  They are all we have, you see,
    all we have to fight off
      illness and death.

Incorporating the stories in the narrative makes the novel itself a ceremony, a set of stories aimed at healing the fractured lives of her people.

Momaday, impressed with Silko's use of the 'telling,' employs the form in *The Ancient Child*, a book that infuses Kiowa myth into a realistic novel. This interchange – Silko borrows Momaday's psychically damaged veteran; Momaday in turn borrows Silko's new form – shows the high degree of awareness of each others' work that Indian writers have. The most relentless borrower from his Indian colleagues was the late Louis Owens (Choctaw/Cherokee). He delighted in paying *hommage* to fellow Indian writers by putting their characters into his novels. In *Bone Game* (1994) alone, there are allusions to Momaday's Juan Reyes Fragua, Welch's Pretty Weasel, Silko's Emo, Vizenor's Evil Gambler, and Erdrich's Gordie Kashpaw.

In discussing Indians' relationship to their lands, it is important to mention that the sacred nature of the land is related to the traditional tribal views concerning indigenous spirits who live there. Although contemporary authors may not hold these beliefs personally any longer, they still employ them as the basis of their fictive worlds. As a result, the literary geography of Indian fiction has a supernatural dimension. Gerald Vizenor uses the term 'mythic verism' to describe events in his work like the metamorphosis of a man into a bear. Louis Owens calls Erdrich's use of a fantastic dimension in her work 'mythic realism,' and cites Gabriel Garcia Marquez's 'magical realism' as its source. The basis of both South American and Native American magical realism lies in the conflict between traditional tribal and modern Western beliefs. What critic Amaryll Chanady says of South American writers can be applied to American Indian authors as well:

The presence of the supernatural is often attributed to the primitive or 'magical' Indian mentality, which coexists with European rationality . . . Magical realism is thus based on reality, or a world with which the author is familiar, while expressing the myths and superstitions of the American Indians. (pp. 11,19)

Although Chanady's point is valid about the different mentalities at work in Indian fiction, her language is deplorable: it is gratuitous and insulting to call people who believe in a world peopled by spirits 'superstitious,' and misleading to call them 'primitive.' In much of America many of the people who believe the world is full of spirits – and only 6,000 years old – are evangelical Christians, and they are far more likely to be white than Indian. Most Indians today believe in the scientific paradigm. If Silko gets sick, she sees a doctor, not a shaman. Nonetheless, for the purposes of literature, Indian writers employ the traditional tribal beliefs. In some cases the writers actually hold the beliefs; in others they treat them as valid within the world of their novels.

To move to the second of the related points, the use of tribal traditions, basing modern novels on myths and on the archetypal characters which appear in tribal tales, is quite common among Indian writers. Far and away the most important archetype in traditional tribal tales is the trickster, the cultural hero of virtually all North American tribes.[15]

Gerald Vizenor is the writer who first comes to mind when the trickster is mentioned. Vizenor is a trickster who writes novels about tricksters in the hope of inculcating trickster values in his readers. His first novel, *Darkness in Saint Louis Bearheart*, is a frame tale in which a trickster, Saint Louis Bearheart, steals time from his Bureau of Indian Affairs job to write a science fiction novel about a group of tricksters who try to survive in America after the country has literally run out of gas, and the government is commandeering reservation trees for fuel.

The principal leader of the band of tricksters in *Bearheart*, Proude Cedarfair, has a climactic showdown with a common tribal villain, the Evil Gambler. Vizenor came across the Evil Gambler in Chippewa tales,[16] but he also figures in Pueblo mythology, and Silko includes a story about him in *Ceremony*. Proude's credo,

> Outwit but never kill evil . . . evil revenge is blind and cannot be
> appeased by the living. The tricksters and warrior clowns have
> stopped more evil violence with their wit than have lovers with their
> lust and fools with the power and rage . . .[17]

is not always the trickster ethic, since there are many Indian tricksters with blood on their hands. For instance, Nanabozho kills a monster called the Windigo who has been terrorizing the Chippewa. And Proude himself is responsible for the death of the Evil Gambler. Vizenor has a point, however, since tricksters are primarily comic figures who refuse to be serious even in the face of evil. They view life as a game. As Vizenor puts it, 'the trickster is a comic liberator in a narrative . . .'[18]

Vizenor has inveighed against social science formulations about the nature of the trickster, but it seems fair to say that the trickster is a reification of the Saturnalian spirit, more interested in ignoring authority and indulging his appetites than in fighting evil. When called upon, the trickster does his duty to his tribe and faces up to evil, but he uses his wit and keeps his sense of humor.

Vizenor may have been the first Indian novelist to base a character on the trickster, but the practice has become common. Louise Erdrich is also Chippewa, and her trickster, Gerry Nanapush, is, like Vizenor's Proude Cedarfair, an avatar of Manabozho. In fact, Nanapush is a variant of the name Manabozho, since transliteration of Chippewa terms varies quite a bit. Gerry is an escape artist who appears in three of Erdrich's novels. Like the archetypal Trickster, Gerry plays tricks, and is the victim of tricks. He is a figure of enormous appetites and zest for life. Beyond good and evil, he violates society's laws and taboos, yet remains sympathetic to the reader. As his stepfather Beverly Lamartine puts it in *Love Medicine*, Gerry is 'both a natural criminal and a hero.'[19]

Gerry has spent much of his life in prison, his chief offense being breaking out. Despite his enormous bulk – he is 6 feet four inches tall, and weighs 320 pounds – he is able to disappear from a restaurant, leap from a third-story window without being hurt, hide in a car trunk, and break into an apartment by climbing up a skylight shaft. Gerry manages to get his wife Dot pregnant in the visiting room of a prison, hiding in the corner that the close-circuit camera cannot reach. Gerry is last seen in *Tales of Burning Love*, Erdrich's fifth novel in the *Little No Horse* series. He has broken out of prison, and is dressed in drag to escape the notice of the police. Gender-bending is common in trickster tales; in fact, at times the trickster is androgynous. Wakdjunkaga (Winnebago) carries the trick furthest, making himself a vagina out of an elk's liver, marrying the chief's son and actually bearing several children before he is found out.[20]

Many Indian writers flavor their works with phrases from their tribal languages in order to give them an atmosphere of ethnic authenticity. The ability of Indians to speak their traditional languages has waned in the past half century. The early twentieth-century government policy of making Indians speak only English failed badly; despite severe corporal punishment at boarding schools, Indians kept speaking their tribal languages.

When the government abandoned this cruel policy, the desire to assimilate accomplished what force could not: Indians found to their dismay that their children often resisted learning their traditional languages, preferring to speak English.[21] Now, for the most part, only Indians in their sixties or older are fluent in traditional languages.

To combat the loss of languages, tribes and universities in western states have instituted language programs and courses. The University of Oklahoma, for instance, teaches Cherokee, Choctaw, Kiowa, and Creek. Few major Indian novelists speak much of their traditional language, though many use phrases in their work. For instance, Gerald Vizenor employs a number of Chippewa phrases in his works, and Thomas King, a mixed-blood Cherokee, uses Cherokee chapter headings in his novel *Green Grass Running Water*,[22] although the book is primarily about the Blackfoot. Louise Erdrich has been learning Chippewa, and she increasingly makes use of it in her novels. In her first book, *Love Medicine*, she employed only a few Indian words, and these were Cree, which was the *lingua franca* of Turtle Mountain reservation.[23] In the last novel in the *Machimanito* series, *Last Report of the Miracles at Little No Horse*, Erdrich used paragraph-long passages of Chippewa.

Perhaps the most interesting use of a traditional tribal language in a contemporary Indian novel occurs in the late James Welch's *Fools Crow* (1986), a historical novel set in Montana in the second half of the nineteenth century when the Blackfeet were still an independent nation, not yet conquered by the US Cavalry.[24] Naturally they spoke Blackfeet, and Welch had the problem of all historical novelists, film-makers and others: how to give characters a language that somehow represents their culture but is still apprehensible to the reader or audience. Directors of westerns have traditionally resorted to very formal English, devoid of contemporary colloquialisms, delivered by unsmiling Tonto figures in a dreary monotone. The most successful writers of historical novels construct a dialect that is essentially English but is littered with enough foreign terms that it seems authentic. In *Waverley*, for instance, Walter Scott peppered the dialect of his Scots characters with a few Highland terms like 'droghling coghling bailie,' and left the final consonant off a few words (o') to give the flavor of Highland speech.[25]

Welch pretty much follows Scott's example. He writes essentially standard English, but adds to it some Blackfeet words – *Kis-see-no-o* (coyote) – and a larger number of literal translations from Blackfeet like 'many-faces man' or 'white man's water' to give the flavor of Blackfeet speech. Welch is a highly skilled writer, with a fine ability to portray contemporary speech, so he succeeds in giving an air of verisimilitude to *Fools Crow*.

The American Indian literary renaissance includes an explosion in the publication of poetry as well as prose. In fact, Indian writers are unique among American writers in that they have been successful in more than one genre. Momaday, Welch, Silko, Vizenor, Erdrich, and Alexie all began as poets. Momaday and Vizenor have had plays produced, and Alexie has written one film (*Smoke Signals*) and written and directed another (*The Business of Fancydancing*, also the title of a collection of poems by Alexie).

Scott Momaday began his writing career as a poet, and in fact originally planned to make *House Made of Dawn* a suite of poems rather than novel.[26] Momaday studied with Yvor Winters at Stanford, and his early poems, like Winters', are heavy on Latinate diction. Typical of this sort of poetry is his description of a mouse: 'His frailty discrete, the rodent turns, looks,' ('Buteo Regalis') and a snake: 'His cordate head meanders through himself:/ Metamorphosis' ('Pit Viper').[27] However, soon Momaday moved to the repetitive rhythms of traditional Indian songs:

Remember my horse running
   Remember my horse
Remember my horse running
   Remember my horse.

Remember my horse wheeling
   Remember my horse
Remember my horse wheeling
   Remember my horse.[28]

James Welch, the Blackfeet writer who came into prominence shortly after Momaday did, introduced surrealism into Indian verse. 'Magic Fox' is perhaps the best example. The poem begins:

They shook the green leaves down,
those men that rattled
in their sleep. Truth became
a nightmare to their fox.
He turned their horses into fish,
Or was it horses strung
like fish, or fish like fish
hung naked in the wind.[29]

Explicating surrealistic poems is a questionable enterprise, but it would seem that 'Magic Fox' is about dreaming. The dreamers – 'those men that rattled in their sleep' – dream of horses and fish in this passage, and later in the poem, stars and a beautiful girl. A trickster in the form of magic fox controls these dreams, causing the dream images to metamorphose.

Surrealism is the art of dreams and dream visions. French in origin, with roots in Dada and Symbolism, it spread through Spain to Latin America. The chief influence on Welch's poetry comes from Peruvian poet Cesar Vallejo, whose works Welch encountered chiefly through the translations of James Wright and Robert Bly. Surrealism appealed to Welch because there is a similarity between the dream visions of some of the surrealists and the dream visions which form the basis of the spiritual life of the Blackfeet and other plains tribes. Welch's novel *Fools Crow* centers on the experiences of a hero whose life is guided by his dreams through the intervention of an animal helper. Welch's poem 'Getting Things Straight' describes a hawk, and ends with the line: 'Is he my vision?'[30]

In Welch's poetry the dreams are often malevolent or threatening. 'Picnic Weather' begins:

> I know the songs we sang,
> the old routine, the dozen masks
> you painted when we left you
> alone, afraid, frightened of yourself
> the day the bull snakes rose,
> seething out of dreams, has made you
> what you are – alone, afraid, stronger.[31]

Here the snakes that rise seething from dreams seem to symbolize dark, frightening sexual threats from within the mind itself.

Sherman Alexie, the best of the Indian writers of the second generation of the Indian renaissance, shows the influence of Welch in his verse. As Kent Chadwick put it in a review of Alexie's collection of poems 'The Business of Fancydancing,' Alexie's writing builds on the naked realism and ironic wonder of . . . James Welch . . . [and] adds a surrealist twist . . .'[32] 'Crazy Horse Speaks' exemplifies this. It begins:

> I discovered the evidence
> In a vault of The Mormon Church
> 3,000 skeletons of my cousins

in a silence so great
I built four walls around it
And gave it a name.
I called it Custer
and he came to me
again in a dream.
He forgave all my sins.

The best of Indian poets are masters of their craft, and students of the past masters in their field. Scott Momaday has a PhD in American Literature from Stanford, where he focused on the reaction against the romantic movement in nineteenth-century America, and particularly the poetry of the period. James Welch studied with Richard Hugo at the University of Montana, getting a thorough grounding in European and Latin American, as well as American, poetry. Sherman Alexie is more of an auto-didact than Momaday or Welch, yet he is thoroughly familiar with poetic tradition. As Chadwick observes: 'In the title poem, "The Business of Fancydancing," Alexie makes striking use of the classical sestina form of Dante and the French Provencal troubadors.'[33] But Indian poets also make use of their own traditions, for example in Alexie's 'Reservation Love Song:'

I can meet you
In Springdale buy you beer
& take you home
in my one-eyed Ford.

Here Alexie is referring to the refrain of a well-known '49' song. These songs, which originated with the Kiowa, are an interesting development showing the vitality and adaptability of Indian cultural forms. The songs are a modern adaptation of the traditional war-journey songs women sang when their loved ones went into battle. The custom of singing '49' songs spread from the Kiowa to all corners of Indian Country. Today groups gather after powwows to sing 49s, which consist of several minutes of vocables, sung to the accompaniment of a drum, culminating with a refrain, generally in English. One of the best known refrains is:

I don't care if you're married I still love you
I don't care if you're married
After the party's over,
I will take you home in my one-eyed Ford.[34]

Diane Burns (Chemehuevi, Chippewa) begins her poem 'Big Fun' with this refrain, and concludes it with another: 'I'm from Oklahoma/I got no one to call my own.'[35] That traditional songs could adapt, survive, and find their way into contemporary poetry is a sign of the dynamic nature of contemporary Indian culture.

Indian drama has not been as successful as fiction and poetry in the United States during the Indian renaissance, although Hanay Geiogamah (Kiowa) has had some success.[36] His scathing but humorous play *Body Indian* was produced off Broadway by LaMama Company in the 1970s.

In conclusion, Indian literature has flourished enormously in the past four decades, to the point where one can say with confidence that it is the full equal of other American ethnic literatures – Jewish, African American, Asian – although its practitioners are not as well known as Saul Bellow, Toni Morrison, or Amy Tan.

NOTES

1. Theoretically, of course, any work by an Indian would qualify as Indian literature, but there seems little point in a course on Indian literature in studying *Gorky Park* by Martin Cruz Smith (Senecu del Sur), since the discussion would have to center on Russian geography and politics rather than on any matter concerning Indians. The same might be said of *The Master Butcher's Singing Club*, the latest novel by Louise Erdrich (Chippewa), since although she is undoubtedly one of the best and best known Indian novelists writing today, the book is primarily about Germans in North Dakota.
2. The principal exception would be the *Walam Olum*, a Delaware epic which was written as a series of pictographs. Some scholars question the authenticity of the poem. For a discussion of the controversy, see Jace Weaver, *That the People Might Live*, p. 48.
3. For a list of Indian novels see Louis Owens, *Other Destinies* (Norman: University of Oklahoma Press, 1992), p. 283ff.
4. Momaday is Kiowa on his father's side, and Cherokee on his mother's.
5. See Owens, *Other Destinies*.
6. The Laguna myths and the Grail myths are remarkably similar in the respect of the linkage between the fate of the hero and his land.
7. Bears were sacred animals to many tribes. See for instance, Momaday's *In the Bear's House* (New York: St Martin's, 1999).
8. Malcolm Cowley, *Exile's Return* (New York: Viking, 1951), p. 13.
9. Indians often practise what is called 'religious dimorphism' – that is, they practise one religion but also hold sacred elements of another.
10. Vine Deloria, Jr, *God is Red* (Golden: North American Press, 1992) pp. 62, 63.
11. Deloria, *God is Red*, p. 67.

7.1 Photograph by Etta Becker-Donner of the rock engravings at the Village of the Great Kiva

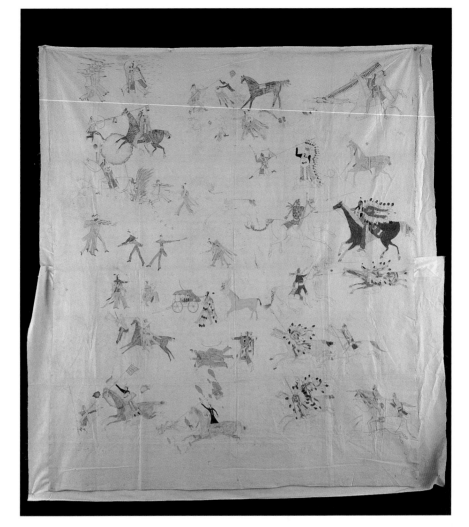

7.2 Silverhorn, 'The Exploits of Sun Boy', c. 1880–1900, The Philbrook Museum of Art, Tulsa, Oklahoma

7.3 Jack Hokeah, 'Portrait of Indian Man', Gilcrease Museum, Tulsa, Oklahoma

7.4 Acee Blue Eagle, 'The Deer Spirit', Heard Museum, Phoenix, Arizona

7.5 Jerome Richard Tiger, 'Endless Trail', 1966, The Philbrook Museum of Art, Tulsa, Oklahoma

7.6 Pablita Velarde, 'Koshares of Taos', The Philbrook Museum of Art, Tulsa, Oklahoma

7.7 Waldo Mootzka, 'Pollination of the Corn', The Philbrook Museum of Art, Tulsa, Oklahoma

7.8 Julian Martinez, 'Pottery Design', Gilcrease Museum, Tulsa, Oklahoma

7.9 Oscar Howe, 'Victory Dance', c. 1954, The Philbrook Museum of Art, Tulsa, Oklahoma

7.10 T. C. Cannon, 'Osage with a Van Gogh or Collector #5', Heard Museum, Phoenix, Arizona

7.11 Otis Polelonema, 'New Bride Woman', Courtesy California Academy of Sciences, San Francisco, California, The Ruth and Charles Elkus Collection, catalog # CAS 0371129

7.12 Fred Beaver, 'The Orator', Heard Museum, Phoenix, Arizona

7.13 Robert Chee, 'On the Way to the Trading Post', c. 1957, The Philbrook Museum of Art, Tulsa, Oklahoma

7.14 Michael Kabotie, 'Petroglyphs', Heard Museum, Phoenix, Arizona

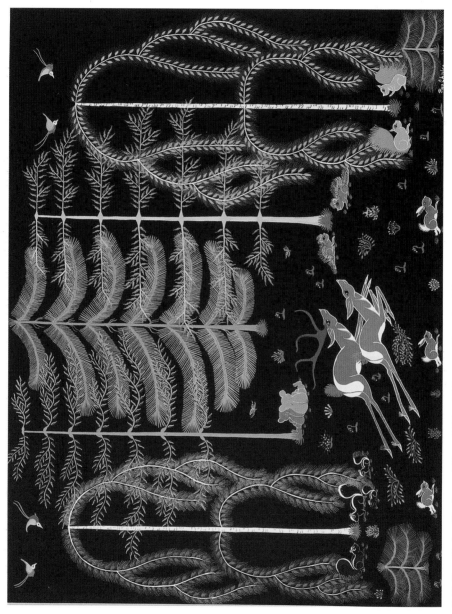

7.15 Pop Chalee, 'Enchanted Forest', Heard Museum, Phoenix, Arizona

7.16 Helen Hardin, 'Recurrence of Spiritual Elements', Heard Museum, Phoenix, Arizona

7.17 Edgar Heap of Birds, 'Reclaim', 1992, Neuberger Museum of SUNY, Purchase, New York

12. Frank Pommersheim, *Braid of Feathers* (Berkeley: University of Californian Press, 1995), p. 13.
13. Frank Pommersheim, *Braid of Feathers*, p. 14
14. Owens, *Other Destinies*, p. 168.
15. See Chapter 2.
16. See Gerald Vizenor, *Narrative Chance* (Albuquerque: University of New Mexico Press, 1989), pp. 126–8.
17. Gerald Vizenor, *Darkness in Saint Louis Bearheart* (St Paul: Truck Press, 1978), p. 11.
18. Vizenor, *Narrative Chance*.
19. Gerald Vizenor, *Love Medicine* (New York: Holt, Rinehart, Winston, 1984), p. 118.
20. Paul Radin, *The Trickster* (New York: Greenwood Press, 1956), p. 22.
21. Other factors like intermarriage also contributed to the decline. See Chapter 4 for a fuller discussion.
22. Thomas King, *Green Grass Running Water* (New York: Houghton Mifflin, 1993).
23. Patrick Gourneau, *History of the Turtle Mountain Band of Chippewa Indians* (privately printed on Turtle Mountain Reservation, 1971), p. 9
24. In America the tribe uses the word 'Blackfeet;' in Canada they use 'Blackfoot.'
25. Thomas King, *Green Grass Running Water* (New York: Viking Penguin, 1972), p. 307.
26. Matthias Schubnell, *N. Scott Momaday* (Norman: University of Oklahoma Press, 1985), p. 93.
27. Both poems may be found in his collection *Angle of Geese* (Boston: David Godine, 1974), pp. 6, 7.
28. 'Plainview: 2,' in *Angle of Geese*, p. 16
29. For the full text, see James Welch, *Riding the Earthboy 40* (New York: Harper & Row, 1971), p. 3.
30. Welch, *Riding the Earthboy*, p. 53.
31. Welch, *Riding the Earthboy*, p. 12
32. www.english.uius.edu/maps/poets/a_f/alexie/reviews/htm
33. Ibid.
34. For a collection of '49s', see Alan Velie, *American Indian Literature* (Norman: University of Oklahoma Press, 1991), p. 89.
35. Velie, *American Indian Literature*, p. 301.
36. There are several successful Canadian Native dramatists, foremost among them Tomson Highway (Cree).

CHAPTER 7

Indian Aesthetics: Art and Expressive Culture

A sense of aesthetics is essential in contemporary American Indian community life. It may be as simple as the brightly colored shawls that women wear when they dance at community gatherings, or as complex as a painting hanging on a gallery wall. Contemporary Indian art encompasses a range of expressions that includes fine arts, traditional crafts such as beadwork and pottery, and music and dance. There is a phrase that has become almost a cliché in contemporary Indian communities – 'There is no word for art in our language.' The intent is to deny that anything is done simply to be beautiful. The truth of the statement may be taken to mean that producing beautiful objects or performing in beautiful ways is a marker of cultural identity that is still important to Native people. It is in the field of aesthetics, the study of the beautiful, that Indian people have demonstrated perhaps most profoundly their ability to survive and to adapt their sense of innate beauty to new media in their own cultural ways.

PAINTING

Given the diversity of styles, and the contempt occasionally evinced by one school for another, there is room to question the assertion that Indian painting has as distinct a set of aesthetic principles as Indian literature does. Rennard Strickland, a Cherokee law professor and art critic, argues that Indian painters do have a distinctive aesthetic:

> While Indian art has multiple artists and thereby multiple
> intentions, the Indian cultural worldview is the essence of Native

American painting, whether the style is traditionalism or individualism. All speak to an Indian experience in an Indian idiom.[1]

One must always be aware, however, of regional and even tribal differences, as well as stylistic ones, when discussing Indian painting. Nonetheless since similarities outweigh differences, it is possible to make valid generalizations. With Indian painting, as with literature, it is helpful to begin with a brief history.

The earliest North American Indian drawings and paintings that have been preserved are the rock paintings and incised petroglyphs of New Mexico, Arizona, Washington, and Utah.[2] It may seem curious to begin an examination of a highly sophisticated art tradition with a discussion of petroglyphs – one would not begin a discussion of French painting with Lasceaux, for instance – but the traditions begun with the rock paintings remain strong in contemporary Indian art.

For the most part rock art is pictographic; the animals and objects are depicted in a fashion that is more symbolic than representational. In Figure 7.1 we have a petroglyph dating from twelfth-century New Mexico. The animals are stylized, and men are depicted symbolically with sticklike limbs and trunks, and sunlike heads. There are symbolic designs as well, lines and spirals.

Another form of early painting involved the use of animal hides, the earliest example being recorded by Coronado in 1540. In 1805 Lewis and Clark gave Jefferson a buffalo hide painting of a battle fought in the late eighteenth century.[3] Hide paintings are generally pictographic. According to German anthropologist and art historian Christian Feest, the style of painting on hides is a 'form of picture writing' in which aesthetic effect is less important than conveying historical information.[4] Hide paintings may seem to be the essence of pristine Indian art, but early in the nineteenth century Plains Indians had contact with American and European artists, especially George Catlin and Karl Bodmer,[5] and their style began to change, moving away from pictography towards mimetic realism. Indian artists still retained a good deal of stylization: they generally depicted horses with very small heads and very long necks. Often the horses were green or crimson, as well as brown and black.

When Indians settled on reservations, paper, particularly ledger books, and occasionally cloth replaced hides as the medium for paintings. A masterpiece of this style from the late nineteenth century is Figure 7.2, a work in colored pencil, ink and paint on muslin by the Kiowa artist Silverhorn

(Haungooah) dating from 1880–1900. The characteristics that would come to typify the best of the easel paintings of the first years of the twentieth century are already in evidence here: strong sense of line, careful attention to detail, absence of background, a variety of colors, and a developed sense of composition.

Silverhorn has a highly developed sense of style. He is not trying to 'hold the mirror up to nature' and failing because of ineptitude. As Rennard Strickland says of a ledger depiction of another battle:

> The ledger book creator of battlefield Indian riders was not trying to reproduce the Battle of Little Bighorn photographically. These artists are 'reductionists,' painting symbols that go to the essence of being. Indian art may seem clumsy and ineffectual if the viewer believes the Native artist is trying to paint a real horse in the style of a European salon painter. Indian art becomes a highly sophisticated abstraction when the viewer understands why the painter draws transparent horse stacked upon transparent horse. It is not childish gibberish, but a language of philosophical metaphor whereby the artist communicates at a different level of reality.[6]

Ledger art was the inspiration for Indian easel art in the early years of the twentieth century. Silverhorn's nephew, Stephen Mopope, was one of the Kiowa Five, a group of Kiowa men (and initially a woman) who established a style which combined techniques of ledger art with the Art Deco illustrative style popular in mainstream America at the time.[7] The five – Spencer Asah, James Auchiah, Jack Hokeah, Monroe Tsatoke, and Mopope (and for a short while, Lois Smoky) – attended the University of Oklahoma as special students, studying with Edith Mahier and Oscar Jacobson. The Kiowa Five style of art, the 'flat style,' consisted of two-dimensional pictures with, in the words of John Warner, 'opaque colors, clear outlines, sinuous curves, and an emphasis on line.'[8] The Kiowa Five became well known throughout the United States, and even in Europe, where what Warner calls their 'paradigm' became dominant in the Indian art world, and remained so until Fritz Scholder and the Santa Fe school began the American Indian renaissance.

Jack Hokeah's 'Portrait of and Indian Man', shown in Figure 7.3, is a good example of Kiowa Five style. Hokeah presents the figure without perspective against a monochrome background devoid of any objects. Hokeah has a strong sense of line, and uses strong flat colors.

Oscar Jacobson, the Swedish-born head of the University of Oklahoma School of Art, who mentored the Kiowa Five, also taught Acee Blue Eagle (Creek/Pawnee), who became director of Bacone Junior College, an Indian school in Oklahoma. Bacone turned out numerous Indian painters, best known of whom were Woody Crumbo (Creek/Pottawatomi) and Richard West (Cheyenne). Janet Berlo and Ruth Philips credit Bacone (along with Dorthy Dunn's Studio School in Santa Fe) with giving birth to the 'traditional style' of Indian art.[9] Blue Eagle's 'The Deer Spirit' (Figure 7.4) is a good example of this style. In its monochrome background, the symmetry and centrality of a dominant figure, and the geometric patterns evident in the plant life, it owes a good deal to the Kiowa Five. However, Blue Eagle uses more detail in depicting his figures, and moves away from the Kiowa simplicity of line towards more complicated patterns.

Although the most famous painter of what might be called the 'Oklahoma School', Jerome Tiger, did not go to Bacone, he certainly betrays the influence of Blue Eagle and his pupils. His watercolor 'Endless Trail' (Figure 7.5) represents the best of traditional Indian painting. The monochrome, often blue, background is typical of Tiger, whose paintings use an economy of line and detail, and a subtle use of muted color, to evoke a mood very powerfully.

There were talented Indian painters throughout the United States in the years leading up to the Second World War, but in addition to Oklahoma the other important center of the traditional style was Santa Fe, New Mexico. In 1932 Dorothy Dunn, an Anglo from Kansas, established an art program at the Santa Fe Indian School. The 'Studio School' drew on Pueblo traditions, which were substantially different from Plains Indian traditions, with more emphasis on design and less on narrative content. Pueblo Indians had a long tradition of sand painting connected with religious rituals, but sand paintings were essentially designs with little narrative content.

Dunn encouraged her students to 'derive their inspiration from the great artistic traditions that were their heritage – abstract forms painted on pottery, figurative rock art, and geometric beadwork and basketry patterns.'[10] Accordingly, the Santa Fe Studio style is dramatically different from the Oklahoma style. Typically, Santa Fe artists fill their canvases with more figures, and use a great deal more detail in depicting costumes, features, and things in the background.

Santa Clara artist Pablita Velarde's 'Koshares of Taos' (Figure 7.6) has the distinctive look of a New Mexico painting: a multitude of figures rendered in detail, a strong sense of symmetry, the use of solid form and vivid color. Hopi painter Waldo Mootzka's 'Pollination of the Corn' (Figure 7.7) has an even stronger sense of design. The strong symmetry, and the fact that the figures float in an abstract landscape, suggest the patterns of Art Deco, but derive ultimately from the Hopi tradition of kiva mural art.[11] In some cases New Mexico artists simply painted designs. Julian Martinez's water-color 'Pottery Design' (Figure 7.8), transfers to paper the sort of designs he had painted on the pots of his wife Maria, the famous potter of San Ildefonso.

Although Dunn helped to train a large number of successful artists, her insistence on what she considered Pueblo tradition may have stunted the artistic growth of some of her students. Apache painter and sculptor Alan Houser said of her years later:

> She should have given me the chance to study anatomy, for instance. But she said: 'No, Indians have a natural feeling for action and rhythm.' . . . My only objection to Dorothy Dunn was this: she trained us all the same way. 'You either paint like this, Mr Houser, or it's not Indian art.'[12]

Perhaps the most distinguished graduate of the Santa Fe Studio is Sioux artist Oscar Howe. Howe began painting in a traditional style, but after a stint in Europe as a soldier during the Second World War he got an MFA in painting, and made a radical departure to a style that looks like Cubism, but which he insists draws on Sioux traditions. Figure 7.9 is a case in point. It is hard to look at it without thinking of Braque's 'Nude Descending the Stairs,' yet Howe claims that his inspiration is primarily the Sioux trickster Iktomi, or Spider, the 'multifaceted pictorial surfaces [being] a spider-web.'[13] Wherever he got his inspiration, like the Cubists Howe transforms the human body into an assemblage of geometric forms. Howe appropriates ideas from Cubism for the same reason that Mootzka borrows from Art Deco and James Welch employs surrealism: the styles appeal to the artist because they remind him of things central to his tribal traditions. Furthermore, it is important to note that Cubism itself was in part inspired by indigenous art. Rennard Strickland points out: 'The contemporary Indian mirrors the cubist, who mirrors the carver of primitive masks, who mirrors the Native world view.'[14]

When Howe began his new style of painting, he was odd man out in the Indian art scene, which was gaining considerable prominence. In the first half of the twentieth century, few outside of Indian country had experi-enced Indian poetry, music, or dance, and Indians had only published a handful of novels, but Indian painting was well known in the American art world, and even in Europe. In the early 1930s the Exposition of Indian Tribal Arts showed in New York before touring the US and Europe, and in 1941 the Museum of Modern Art devoted three floors to Indian art.[15] After the Second World War the Philbrook Museum in Tulsa began an annual exhibition of Indian art, and its preference for paintings of the Oklahoma and Studio schools acted as a conservative influence. In 1958 the Philbrook rejected a painting of Howe's. His outraged response gave the Philbrook pause, and caused them to liberalize their standards, but to this day the preponderance of their paintings are traditional.

It was a student of Howe's, Luiseno painter Fritz Scholder, who revolutionized Indian painting. In some respects the situation in Indian art is similar to that in Indian literature: in both fields there was a renaissance that began in the 1960s. But there are differences as well. Whereas in literature there was a renaissance in the sense of an efflorescence of literary works, the renaissance in Indian painting involved stylistic changes as radical as that of the European Renaissance from the Middle Ages. While not replacing traditional styles of painting in most Indian art galleries, Santa Fe artists like Fritz Scholder and T. C. Cannon created a new style of Indian painting which brought them to the attention of the American art world much as Momaday, Erdrich, Alexie et al. came to prominence in the American literary scene.

The impetus for the artistic renaissance came from the Rockefeller Foundation conference at the University of Arizona in 1959, in which participants decided that, as John Warner reports, 'Indian art was stagnant or moribund, and "new directions" were needed.'[16] The next year Rockefeller funded the Southwestern Indian Art Project, which operated as a summer program in 1960 and '61. These programs led to the establishment of the Institute of American Indian Arts (IAIA) which opened in Santa Fe in 1962. The students at IAIA established a style of painting that combined techniques of Euro-american modernism with traditional Indian subjects. The Institute hired Fritz Scholder (Luiseno) as an instructor, and the Santa Fe school was soon in full swing. Scholder had studied with Wayne Thiebaud, and appropriated what Edgar Heap of Birds describes as Thiebaud's 'vibrating color and messy gesture,'[17] along with a Pop Art sensibility. Later Scholder discovered Francis Bacon at the Tate, and was moved by Bacon's use of color, simplified forms, and 'monstrous quality.'[18]

Scholder introduced the students at IAIA to artists like Pollock, deKooning, Rothko, Munch, and Bacon, and the Santa Fe School turned away with disdain from what they called the 'Waters of the Minnetonka school,' and 'Bambi Art,'[19] that is, the style passed down by the Kiowa Five.

Scholder, who has lately given up painting Indian subjects, brought a great deal of irreverence to Indian art. In order to smash stereotypes about Indians and Indian art, he painted Indians in traditional dress doing things designed to shock and amuse viewers, and to force them to recognize that Indians are Americans living in the present. He depicts subjects wearing or carrying an American flag, holding a seagull, or eating an ice cream cone.

Scholder's most talented disciple, T. C. Cannon (Caddo/Kiowa), does much the same thing in his painting 'Osage with a Van Gogh' (Figure 7.10). In the early years of the twentieth century the Osage discovered oil on their lands, and soon became the wealthiest people in Oklahoma. They built large houses, and furnished them with grand pianos and expensive paintings.[20] Cannon's painting is humorous, but the joke is based on historical fact.

THE INDIAN AESTHETIC

As with Indian literature, it is possible to speak of an Indian aesthetic in regard to painting, and we will consider the same topics: relationship to land, connection to tribal traditions, relationship to nature in particular and animals in general, and the cyclical nature of time.

To begin with the land: when looking at Indian paintings of any style – ledger art, Oklahoma or Santa Fe Studio School, or paintings of Scholder, Cannon and others – one is struck by the paucity of details in the backgrounds of most pictures. Judging from the detailed descriptions of the landscape in many Indian novels, one would think that Indian paintings would have the background detail of a Breughel or at least a Monet. However, that is not at all the case. In ledger art, figures are shown against an empty background, and the same is true for most pictures by the Kiowa Five (see Figure 7.3). Oklahoma school painters like Acee Blue Eagle and Jerome Tiger generally depict monochrome backgrounds with only a few highly stylized details (Figures 7.4 and 7.5), New Mexico artists like Otis Polelonema (Hopi) (Figure 7.11) set figures against empty backgrounds. Scholder's backgrounds are generally one or two slabs of solid color or occasionally an abstract pattern.

One possibility for the lack of detailed depiction of landscape is tradition. Cherokee art collector and scholar Rennard Strickland posits 'the absence of background in "traditional Indian painting" was a product of what quickly became the "standards" for native painting which drew on ledger, teepee, and pottery decorations styles.'[21] Strickland adds that the flatness of the plains of Oklahoma and eastern New Mexico, and the open horizon added to the tendency to have few details in the background. He claims that painters from woodland areas like Fred Beaver (Creek) and Cecil Dick (Cherokee) believed that 'Woodland painting properly included landscape,' but they felt constrained to follow the canons of the established schools. In some of their works you can see a good deal more background detail than is common in their contemporaries, though it too is stylized and verges on the abstract (Figure 7.12).

Another aspect of tradition is the pressure of white mentors. Cherokee scholar Jace Weaver claims that the problem is that teachers like Oscar Jacobson and Dorothy Dunn felt that the empty background of ledger art represented the true Indian style.[22] And finally, Cheyenne artist Edgar Heap of Birds argues that 'The image of Native art has historically been that of an abstracted image filled with intense conceptual narrative . . . Native visual art is just part of a breathing system and networks with other components in the tribal culture.'[23]

According to Heap of Birds, traditional painters intended their works for tribal audiences who understood the context of their images, which brings us to the point about the Indian aesthetic being dependent on tribal traditions. Tribal members looking at a painting of a dancer would have recognized what ceremony the dancer was performing. Background details would be distracting and irrelevant. Likewise, in paintings like 'On the Way to the Trading Post' (Figure 7.13, by Robert Chee, Navajo), the hills and mesa in the background are suggested in a few lines, not fully depicted. Navajos from the Dine would recognize the mesa as an important place on their land, and putting it alone in the picture instead of drawing it as part of a detailed landscape emphasizes its importance.

For contemporary painters like Scholder, images are also more symbolic and suggestive than mimetic. Scholder's paintings are intended for a well to do white audience, whom he wants to disabuse of the notion that Indians are still living in the nineteenth century, wearing feathers and hunting buffalo. To an extent, the Oklahoma and Santa Fe Studio schools contribute to that misconception, with their tendency to depict scenes of traditional activities. This is one reason Scholder and his disciples have such a strong distaste for what they derisively dismiss as 'Bambi Art.'

Scholder's painting of an Indian in a headdress eating an ice cream cone assaults the white viewer's attitudes about Indians. It tells the viewer that

Indians are not exotic nineteenth-century figures, but Americans partici-
pating in modern life. In a way Scholder's work is an ironic commentary on
photographers like Edward Curtis who made Indians take off wristwatches
or any items of clothing not made of buckskin before he photographed
them. Curtis wanted to show Indians in their pristine state, but that was a
falsification of the way they actually dressed. Scholder attacks this romanticized nostalgia by depicting Indians wearing sunglasses, and wearing or
holding a flag. Background details would only be distracting from the
central images of Scholder's paintings, so he leaves them out. T. C.
Cannon's picture of the Osage collector is more detailed (Figure 7.10), but
the landscape we see outside the window is not rendered with the same
degree of detail as the Osage or his painting.

Tribal traditions are central to Indian painting. Many paintings depict
ceremonies or rituals. Religion is central to Indian life, and dance is often a
religious activity. Paintings of dances and dancers are particularly common.
Archuleta and Strickland's book and collection of paintings and sculptures
Shared Visions has paintings of an Eagle Dance (Alfonso Roybal, San
Ildefonso), Squaw Dance (Harrison Begay, Navajo), Basket Dance (Gilbert
Atencio, San Ildefonso), Sun Dance (Richard West, Cheyenne), Ghost
Dance (Oscar Howe, Sioux) War Dance (Ernest Spybuck, Shawnee), and
White Feather Dance (Joan Hill, Creek). *Shared Visions* also has several
paintings of Indian funerals, weddings, or betrothal ceremonies, as well as
Waldo Mootzka's depiction of the pollination of the corn, Joe Herrera's
'Spring Ceremony for Owah,' and Ernest Smith's painting of Seneca
prophet Handsome Lake declaiming his doctrine.

Indians also cling to Indian traditions not connected to their particular
tribe. Contemporary artists like Michael Kabotie (Hopi) and Sherman
Chaddlestone (Kiowa) have rendered versions of petroglyphs and hide
paintings (Figure 7.14). Figures from traditional narratives are common.
Harry Fonseca (Maidu) has made a career out of depicting southwestern
trickster Coyote in contemporary accoutrements (see cover).

The next point is the Indian relationship to nature in general and animals
in particular. Deer, buffalo and other animals that Indians hunted are particularly common. In fact, the stylized, often cute deer depicted by artists
like Pop Chalee and Maria Lujan Hopkins (Figure 7.15, Taos), to take just
one example, became symbolic of what the postmodern Santa Fe artists,
Scholder, Cannon and others, rebelled against.

The cyclical nature of time is hard to depict in a painting, but many
Indian works seem to suggest it. Paintings like Helen Hardin's 'Recurrence

of Spiritual Elements' (Figure 7.16, Santa Clara) is a case in point. Hardin uses recurring visual motifs to suggest the repetition of temporal patterns. Waldo Mootzka's 'Pollination of the Corn' (Figure 7.7) and Patrick DesJarlait's 'Gathering Wild Rice' use symmetry and repetition to suggest recurring patterns. Finally, the desire of contemporary artists like Kabotie and Chaddlestone to replicate petroglyphs and hide art suggests that times gone by will manifest themselves in the present.

As the twentieth century gave way to the twenty-first, post-modernism, or what Berlo and Phillips call 'post-studio art'[24] began to manifest itself. Post-modern art moves past modernism in freeing itself of the constraints of traditional subjects, materials, and techniques. Highly conceptual, it often has a political edge. Artists like Edgar Heap of Birds (Cheyenne), Colleen Cutschall (Lakota), and Rebecca Belmore (Ojibwa) began constructing installations, using video art, and placing works in public places, not in the traditional way of authorized murals and sculptures, but in an invasive fashion. For instance, some of Heap of Birds' most interesting work is the signs he has designed and installed. He painted a take-off of the infamous Cleveland Indian on a fence near the Indians ballpark, with the message printed underneath: 'SMILE FOR RACISM.' He temporarily installed a series of signs in Norman, Oklahoma that read 'Sooners, today your host is the Cheyenne Tribe' [or a number of other tribes]. Figure 7.17 shows a sign designed for the Neuberger Museum in Purchase, New York.

In conclusion, Indian painting, long better known to the white public than Indian literature or any other art form, is still flourishing, both in the form of traditional styles, and modern and post-modern genres.

Expressive Culture

The establishment of the National Museum of the American Indian at the Smithsonian Institution in 1990 has promoted a new commitment to the study and presentation of 'expressive culture.' The Museum has adopted this rubric for its on-going series of live performances by singers and musicians, demonstrations of crafts, storytelling sessions, and lectures and symposia devoted to showcasing the vitality of contemporary cultural expressions.[25]

American Indian music and dance has been the object of fascination for scholars and tourists alike for decades, but early and even fairly recent scholarly studies were generally done either from an anthropological per-

spective or from a purely musicological perspective.[26] Contemporary scholarship on expressive culture focuses on the individuals who produce the
expression rather than simply its cultural content.

The opening suite of exhibitions at the National Museum of the
American Indian's facility at the George Gustav Heye Center in New York
City included one entitled 'All Roads are Good.' The exhibition catalog was
not a catalog in the traditional object-oriented sense. Instead, it recorded the
process by which Native people from a number of different communities
were invited to the Museum's old storage facility in the Bronx to select
objects for display. The selection process was extensively documented on
videotape, and the exhibit labels, as well as video clips of the selectors in
touchscreen kiosks, were edited from the tapes. The book based on the
exhibit, *All Roads are Good*, featured essays by the selectors that dealt not
just with the objects but with their personal meanings.[27] This emphasis on
the personal experience rather than on the performance per se is evident in
other recent scholarly works. Scholarship is much more collaborative, and
Native people emerge as individuals rather than as 'informants.'[28]

Like painting, sculpture, and other kinds of expressions in the fine arts,
music and dance demonstrate very clearly how contemporary Indian communities have adapted to changing conditions. Christian hymns sung in
Native languages are important evidence of the use of outside influences in
uniquely Native ways.[29] Perhaps the most adaptive forms of expressive
culture is the modern pow-wow. Although some people might view the
pow-wow as a conglomerate of musical and dance styles that diminishes
some innate authenticity of Native ceremonies, it is a vital part of community life in virtually all parts of the country. Accounts of the origins of the
pow-wow reveal the dynamic interactions of cultural groups.[30] Intertribals,
dances that invite participants and spectators alike into the arena, epitomize
the intercultural nature of the pow-wow and the role it plays in promoting
a sense of pan-tribal identity.

People who espouse a pop-culture view of Indians generally assume that
the pow-wow is the truly Indian form of music and dance. The National
Museum of the American Indian's expressive culture series is intended to
educate the public concerning the diversity of forms among Indian tribes
across the United States.[31] Because music and dance are evocative rather
than purely rational, they provide unique insight into cultures. They
provide an opportunity for experiential learning outside the classroom.
Indeed, becoming part of an engaged audience may allow a student to
develop a much deeper understanding of the significance of expressive

culture. The interaction of performers and viewers becomes immediate. The literal meaning of the words of a '49' song may be lost, but the sly humor and innuendo may come through quite clearly.

Music and dance are integral parts of life in Native communities. They are part of the vitality of contemporary cultures. They demonstrate the adaptability of cultural expression. That a Creek Indian woman who is a poet, Joy Harjo, plays the saxophone, leads a band named Poetic Justice, and has written a song about the slain Micma'q activist Annie Mae Aquash, should not be surprising. That Indian teenagers listen to Native rock groups such as Redbone and Indigenous is not surprising either. That they may enjoy those groups, listen to the music of Joy Harjo, and participate in pow-wows, round dances, and tribal ceremonials will seem perfectly natural to the student of expressive culture.

NOTES

1. Rennard Strickland, *Tonto's Revenge* (Albuquerque: University of New Mexico Press, 1997), p. 66.
2. Christian Feest, *Native Arts of North America* (London: Thames and Hudson, 1980), pp. 91–5.
3. Edwin L. Wade, *The Arts of the North American Indian* (New York: Hudson Hills, Press, 1986), p. 56.
4. Feest, *Native Arts*, p. 51.
5. Ibid., p. 57
6. Strickland, *Tonto's Revenge*, p. 67.
7. Wade, *The Arts of the North American Indian*, p. 190.
8. John Warner, 'Contemporary Native American arts: traditionalism and modernism,' *The Journal of Intercultural Studies*, no. 24, 1997, p. 45
9. Janet Berlo and Ruth Phillips, *Native North American Art* (Oxford: Oxford University Press, 1998), p. 217.
10. Berlo and Phillips, *Native North American Art*, p. 217.
11. Wade, *The Arts of the North American Indian*, p. 192.
12. W. Jackson Rushing III, *Native American Art in the Twentieth Century* (London: Routledge, 1999), p. 66.
13. Berlo and Phillips, *Native North American Art*, p. 222.
14. Strickland, *Tonto's Revenge*, p. 69.
15. Berlo and Phillips, *Native North American Art*, p. 218.
16. Warner, 'Contemporary Native American Arts,' p. 72.
17. Email to Alan Velie, 27 May 2003.
18. Adelyn D. Breeskin, 'Introductory,' in *Scholder/Indians* (Flagstaff, AZ: Northland Press, 1972), p. 5.

19. Ibid., p. 1.
20. For a picture of the Osage high life, read Charles Red Corn's *A Pipe for February* (Norman: University of Oklahoma Press, 2002).
21. Email to Alan Velie, 14 May 2003.
22. Email to Alan Velie, 16 May 2003.
23. Email to Alan Velie, 20 May 2003.
24. Berlo and Phillips, *Native North American Art*, p. 234.
25. *Native American Expressive Culture* (Washington, DC, National Museum of the American Indian; Ithaca, NY: Cornell University, 1992).
26. Examples of the anthropological approach are David P. McAllester, *Peyote Music* (New York: Viking Fund, 1949); Charlotte Johnson Frisbie, *Kinaaldá: A Study of the Navajo Girl's Puberty Ceremony* (Middletown: Wesleyan University Press, 1967); Frank Speck and Leonard Broom, in collaboration with Will West Long, *Cherokee Dance and Drama* (Norman: University of Oklahoma Press, 1983). The work of Frances Densmore, *The American Indians and their Music* (New York: Johnson Reprint Corp., 1970, 1926) represents the more strictly musicological approach, although Densmore did gather extensive cultural information about the music she recorded. See also James H. Howard, and Victoria Lindsay Levine, *Choctaw Music and Dance* (Norman: University of Oklahoma Press, 1990).
27. *All Roads are Good* (Washington: Smithsonian Institution Press, in association with the National Museum of the American Indian, 1992).
28. Virginia Giglio, *Southern Cheyenne Women's Songs* (Norman: University of Oklahoma Press, 1994); Judith Vander, *Songprints: The Musical Experience of Five Shoshone Women* (Urbana and Chicago: University of Illinois Press, 1988/1996); Luke E. Lassiter, *The Power of Kiowa Song: A Collaborative Ethnography* (Tucson: University of Arizona Press, 1998).
29. Michael McNally, *Ojibwe Singers: Hymns, Grief, and a Native Culture in Motion* (Oxford: Oxford University Press, 2000); Lisa Philips Valentine, *Making It Their Own: Severn Ojibwe Communicative Practice* (Toronto: University of Toronto Press, 1995).
30. Clyde Ellis, *A Dancing People: Powwow Culture on the Southern Plains* (Lawrence: University Press of Kansas, 2003); Tara Browner, *Heartbeat of the People: Music and Dance of the Northern Pow-wow* (Urbana: University of Illinois Press, 2002).
31. Charlotte Heth (ed.), *Native American Dance: Ceremonies and Social Traditions* (Washington, DC: National Museum of the American Indian Smithsonian Institution with Starwood Publishing Inc., 1994).

CHAPTER 8

The Current Status of Native American Studies

Native American and American Indian Studies programs have created a new body of scholarship that has taken its place in the curricula of academic institutions throughout the country. These programs often began in political confrontation between University administrators and student activists who challenged the premises of traditional disciplines. The advocates of these programs and the courses that they engendered were often subject to charges of political advocacy, an idea that conflicted with the presumed objectivity of traditional disciplines. The nature of objectivity has, however, been the ongoing source of intellectual debate that has made the modern University a marketplace for new ideas.

Native American Studies programs have persisted despite the benign neglect of university administrators, and they have both promoted new scholarship and benefited from the work of non-Indian scholars who have written from new perspectives.

The Ford Foundation has been a major supporter of the development of Native American Studies programs. It provided funding for the development of the Master's degree programs in American Indian Studies established at the University of California at Los Angeles in 1982 and the University of Arizona in 1983. These programs gave further legitimacy to the field. In 1976, the University of California at Berkeley established an Ethnic Studies Ph.D. program with a faculty whose training was all in traditional disciplines. The students came from variously disciplinary backgrounds – English, Political Science, History – and although the Ethnic Studies curriculum was supposed to develop comparative studies, students generally focused on one particular ethnic group and one specific methodology. By default, then,

Ethnic Studies at Berkeley became a route to doctoral level scholarship on American Indian topics. In 1996 the University of Arizona established the first American Indian Studies Ph.D. program in the nation. In 1995 the University of Oklahoma, in a state that is currently home to thirty-nine federally recognized tribes, established an interdisciplinary bachelor's degree program in Native American Studies, and in 2003 the Native American Studies program gained approval for a master's degree. Montana State University established a new graduate program focused on Education in 1997, and the University of California at Davis established master's and doctoral degree programs in 2000.

Some idea of the status of American Indian/Native American programs can be gained from a Commission for Higher Education survey of Indian studies programs. Of the 170 institutions contacted, 100 responded. The programs they described ranged in scope from one or two courses taught in history or anthropology or education departments, and perhaps a counselor with some special responsibility for Indian student concerns, to fully fledged departments with their own faculty and degree programs such as the American Indian Studies Department at Minnesota and the Native American Studies program in the Ethnic Studies Department at the University of California at Berkeley.[1]

By the early 1980s many of the programs that had begun with such optimism and potential promise in the early 1970s had shrunk considerably or disappeared entirely. A survey of 107 institutions conducted in 1980–1 by the American Indian Culture and Research Center at UCLA received responses from only fifty-seven institutions, from which we can infer that although new programs had emerged, many programs that existed in 1976–7 had changed or disappeared by 1981.[2] The political rhetoric used to justify Ethnic Studies departments or programs in general had shifted from the idea of civil rights and affirmative action in the 1970s to the need to educate minority students to meet growing shortages of people available for skilled jobs in an increasingly technological society, and the emphasis in minority recruitment to college programs shifted rather markedly to science majors.[3]

American Indian Studies programs at major universities suffered from the vagaries of academic politics during the 1970s and 1980s. At Minnesota, the department of American Indian Studies was dismantled after a period of turmoil in the urban Indian community over the appointment of a new director. Its faculty were distributed throughout other departments, although it finally regained its standing first as a subset of the American

Studies program and finally its autonomy in the early 1990s. At the University of California at Davis, the Native American Studies degree program was suspended for a time when faculty retirements seemed to threaten the stability of the department. It too regained its status, and has gone on to develop into one of the largest full departments in the country. At Berkeley, the effect of State Proposition 13, which froze property tax rates and hence the state's budget for education, was to force the three programs in the Ethnic Studies Department – Chicano Studies, Asian American Studies, and Native American Studies – into competition for increasingly scarce resources, and in the mid-1990s, as a result of budget cuts and internal turmoil, the administration suspended the search for two faculty positions in Native American Studies left vacant by retirements and resignations.

The survival of Native American/American Indian studies programs during the 1970s and 1980s depended generally on strong leadership by individual faculty and active support by at least one University administrator. New deans often find a program to foster in order to develop their own reputations for nurturing new fields of scholarship, and some Native American/American Indian studies programs have grown because of this fact. But the faculties have learned the skills of academic administration, and the body of scholarship that we have described has had time to grow and mature into the recognizable discipline it has become.

The current status of Native American/American Indian programs can be assessed by reference to the directory of Native American Studies Programs in the United States and Canada, edited by Robert M. Nelson, professor of English at the University of Richmond. The directory currently lists seventy-nine programs in the United States, nine in Canada, and sixteen additional programs that did not provide any information for the guide. Of those programs that responded, thirty-four granted the bachelor's degree, fifty-six had a minor program, and twenty-four listed a concentration. Twenty institutions listed a graduate degree in Native American Studies, although several indicated that such a degree was a concentration in a discipline.

It is interesting that the maturation of the field has occurred primarily through graduate, rather than undergraduate, programs. The interdisciplinary nature of the field lends itself better to the more focused aspect of graduate study. Undergraduate programs have been successful primarily because interdisciplinary study fits the liberal arts model of college education. In terms of allocation of resources, universities have had to balance the demands of offering classes for relatively small numbers of American Indian undergraduates with the opportunity of using faculty expertise to develop future professionals and faculty members. Universities that have established graduate programs have generally not invested resources in undergraduate programs.

Some of the most interesting work in Native American Studies currently is being done at the Tribally Controlled Community Colleges. These thirty-four institutions (as of January 2004) in the United States, and one in Canada, have grown from the movement initiated by the first tribally chartered college, Navajo Community College, which was established in 1968. The Colleges have received federal support under special Congressional legislation, the Tribally Controlled College Assistance Act, as well as support from tribal councils. Reservation-based colleges are unique institutions that meet the needs of their own particular communities. Most offer some curriculum that addresses the specific language(s) and culture(s) of the reservation. Little Big Horn Community College (the Crow Reservation in Montana), Dull Knife Community College (Northern Cheyenne), and Dinè College (Navajo) are excellent examples of colleges with well developed Native Studies programs. Dinè College has adopted a philosophy of education based on traditional Navajo principles of thinking that permeates its entire curriculum.

Four of the colleges are multitribal in their orientation. Haskell Indian Nations University in Lawrence, Kansas, Southwest Indian Polytechnic Institution in Albuquerque, New Mexico, and the Institute of American Indian Arts in Santa Fe, New Mexico, are primarily federally funded institutions which have Indian boards of trustees but are not chartered by a particular tribe. D-Q University in Davis, California serves students from approximately seventy-five tribes and operates under an all-Indian board of trustees. Although the colleges emphasize basic education and job skills, all share a commitment to preparing students to go on to higher degree programs if they choose, and to varying degrees they promote research and creative work on cultural issues. Goodman's *Lakota Star Lore*, for instance, is based on interviews with Lakota tribal elders, and *The Sacred*, by Beck and Walters, was one of the early compilations of tribal traditions that has proven of enduring use in teaching courses on Native American world views.

Because the tribally controlled colleges serve particular constituencies – that is, students from reservation communities (although their student bodies are not exclusively tribal members or even Indians) – their programs in Native cultural studies have particular strengths in local resources for the study of language, culture, and history in an integrated manner, as we have suggested. Because the colleges operate under tribal charters but are governed by independent boards, they have largely been able to protect their academic freedom while still responding to community needs.

The continued support of Native American Studies in tribally controlled community colleges and both state and private colleges and Universities demonstrates that both tribes and American universities have acknowledged Native American/American Indian studies as a legitimate field of academic study. The challenge for the continued development of Native American Studies programs is that the scholarship upon which they depend still comes largely from specific disciplinary perspectives – literary criticism in English departments; history in departments where strict adherence to written documents is still the norm; anthropology departments that emphasize theoretical constructs of culture.

The Native American and non-Native graduate students who have chosen to pursue doctoral studies face unique challenges. Although they may find supportive mentors in certain departments, they are held to standards of scholarship that reflect institutional values and norms. When they come with specific ideas about the kind of research that they feel needs to be done for the benefit of their communities, they may meet with resistance from faculty advisors. If a student has a predetermined conclusion, the advisor has reason to believe that the research cannot be objective. The future of the discipline of Native American studies depends upon the development of new methods in the training of graduate students, methods that will balance the demands of the academy for objective research with the culturally-based knowledge of community needs that Native students bring to universities.

The challenge to Native American Studies programs is to create a truly interdisciplinary curriculum. One of the intellectual strengths of multidisciplinary programs is that students learn a variety of ways of thinking about a single subject. As we have argued in our chapter on cultural contact, knowledge is culturally based. In the academy, knowledge is based in academic disciplines, analogous to different cultures. Disciplines are based on certain assumptions about the nature of human knowledge. Students should be able to understand how different academic disciplines approach the subject of study and they should be able to use the methods of different disciplines. It may seem obvious, for instance, for a community to gain knowledge of its past from oral traditions, from archaeological evidence, from early ethnographic studies, and from written historical accounts. A study engaged in recovering that history must, however, go to sources labeled 'Folklore,' 'Archaeology,' 'Anthropology,' and 'History,' and discover that the information is presented in quite different ways. Students must, however, learn how to cut across these disciplinary boundaries to frame their arguments in new ways.

Throughout this book we have suggested that there are key intellectual issues that have shaped the field and that continue to be matters of debate within the academic world. The underlying one is the issue of scholarly objectivity versus advocacy. By proposing a new set of categories within which to discuss American Indian history, culture, and political issues, we hope both to challenge existing disciplinary assumptions and to propose new ways of raising questions. We do advocate an intellectual stance that values an understanding of opposing viewpoints in order to assure that Native voices, which have not been attended to before, are heard equally with non-Native voices. This position is certainly not unique to American Indian Studies but falls more broadly under rubrics of social history, the 'New Western History,' and post-colonialism and culture studies in literary criticism. We propose it as a critical premise for American Indian Studies.

The academic discipline of history is especially problematic because of its insistence upon the criterion of objectivity, and although that criterion has been held up to critical scrutiny itself in the profession, it is still a standard by which scholarship is judged.[4] History is among the oldest of the academic disciplines, and as such is particularly the product of a time and place and way of thinking. In this respect, the challenge to the scholar doing Indian 'history' is to be quite clear in defining his or her assumptions about what that history is and how it differs from other versions of some historical 'truth.' For example, a basic question that must be asked of oral traditions, and answered, is: when can one person's unique anecdote be taken as historical fact? Or can it? Students must master the techniques of interviewing and analyzing oral narratives that are essential to the field of oral history and they must maintain that degree of skepticism that is inherent in Indian languages – differentiating between experiential knowledge and hearsay, and they must learn to evaluate hearsay for what it can tell us about collective memory and the uses to which it can be put to recover community history.

Our premise concerning tribal sovereignty raises the challenge that it is something we present as a given, not something that we feel must be proven. In that regard, our position can be seen as a political one, even as advocacy, but the important point is that those who oppose tribal sovereignty should see that they speak from a political position rather than a purely objective one. The two viewpoints on sovereignty, that it is inherent in a people because of their occupancy of the land and their powers of self-government, or that it is delegated by the US Congress, have coexisted, have been argued extensively, and, in the end, are philosophical statements rather than matters of fact. The on-going discussions and challenges around the subject will, we hope, strengthen Native communities in their abilities to defend their rights.

Another issue is how American Indian/Native American Studies programs should balance objectives of cultural preservation and cultural adaptation. Language programs, for example, are often viewed as an aspect of cultural preservation, but the possibility is remote that languages that are largely moribund can become functional in daily life in communities. As we argue, the study of languages is a useful tool for understanding different ways of thinking, and students who learn some level of conversational ability and literacy in their particular Native languages may enhance a sense of pride and identification with the tribal group. It is not, however, the role of the university to teach aspects of Native cultures so that students are more competent in practising them but rather to teach students the skills of inquiry that will allow them to recover information where possible and to utilize it in appropriate ways. Native languages stress the act of speaking as a creative act in itself. If students can speak, they may find creative ways of bringing new forms of community life and culture into existence. We stress arts and literature as ways of adapting values and ideas to new media and new forms of expression, rather than strictly as forms of cultural preservation.

Finally, American Indian/Native American Studies programs must confront the issue of defining American Indian identity as an intellectual construct from which to begin their studies. The questions of who and what is an Indian continue to be at the heart of the academic enterprise and increasingly at the core of scholarship.[5] Identity can be blood, it can be culture, it can be language, it can be political membership – the question of identity has many dimensions, and the challenge is to explore all of those dimensions without becoming caught up in the argument that all Indians must have something in common that is the core of identity. Given the diversity of groups, historical experiences, locations, and political issues, questions of identity will remain the source of stimulating and challenging discussions rather than dogmatic doctrines.

By proposing a new set of premises as the basis for American Indian Studies programs, we seek to create a holistic view of cultural life. Although we explore each premise separately, we hope that the reader will see the interconnectedness of the ideas we present. Land (the totality of the environment) is the source of spirituality. It is also the source of sovereignty. The preservation of rights to access sacred places is an issue both of spiritual survival and of sovereign rights to a land base. Sacred places have sacred names which in Native languages are sources of power, both spiritual and social power, as when place names have social and moral implications. The places have stories attached to them which constitute bodies of oral traditions that explain people's association with the land, hence, their history. That history becomes, in turn, a rich source for contemporary authors and artists, who draw inspiration from it and, often, from the physical landscapes that are the source of their own cultural identity. It is these connections that unify the field of American Indian/Native American studies into a coherent, intellectual field of study.

American Indians have found ways of expressing their cultures in artistic forms. Although the statement 'there is no term for art in Indian languages' has become a catchphrase in current Indian political rhetoric, Indian artists and writers have given new expression to Indian traditions and demonstrated the adaptability of their cultures to American society.

As the academic world meets the challenge of new ideas, Native American studies has introduced another perspective into the academy. Indeed, the tension between new and established ideas remains the great excitement of the academy. The contribution of Native communities to the debate is in the fact that they still preserve much of their knowledge in oral traditions, perhaps not so much in origin stories because of the loss of Native language, but in their memories of historical events. Although such knowledge has traditionally had validity in the field of folklore, it has generally been suspect in the field of history. Studies of the history of American Indians communities have, however, introduced new ways of interpreting historical actions.

In the field of anthropology, the development of Native American Studies has challenged the paradigm of acculturation. The idea that one cultural system can completely replace another has given way before the obvious dynamic of cultural change in multicultural societies. New interpretations of culture acknowledge that it is a dynamic rather than a static concept.

In newly emerging academic fields such as women's studies and gender studies, the culturally significant role of the cross-gendered or 'two spirited' person, who takes on the social role of the opposite sex, has received scholarly attention.[6] Women's roles in various Indian societies have become the subject of study.[7]

Native American Studies has engendered a number of publications that have contributed to the definition of the field.[8] These anthologies are examples of new interpretations that enrich the teaching of Native American studies. Other scholarly studies have established new areas of critical inquiry. One is the historical study of Native American intellectuals who critiqued traditional tribal values and explored the possibilities of adaptation to new circumstances.[9]

One of the most important issues for Native American Studies in establishing its distinctiveness as a field of study has been to define the audience for its scholarship. From its initial stance of challenging stereotypes and calling attention to the absence of Indians in history books, Native American Studies has challenged the standards of scholarly research. But scholars in the field have also defined Native communities as their primary audiences. They have introduced standards of ethics in research and a sense of responsibility to native communities.

Indians have been subjects of scholarly study. Their own stories have not been given their due. American Indian scholars who write about their own communities, however, have a particular responsibility to those communities. Non-Indian scholars must also observe standards of ethics that respect the validity of Native knowledge. They must respect the wishes of Native communities with regard to subject of their studies. Weaver and Cook-Lynn stress this responsibility of scholars to their own communities. Weaver explicates a principal of 'comunitas' and Cook-Lynn castigates scholars who act from purely individual motives.[10]

This assertion of communal values and responsibility to community in Native American Studies is an important issue in the development of a methodology that distinguishes the field from others in an academic environment. In 1975, a member of the history department faculty at the University of California at Berkeley characterized a course titled Native American Sovereignty as 'tendentious,' arguing that it was a statement of belief rather than an objective theory to be tested. We assert that that must be taken as a given in Native American Studies.

Native American Studies as an academic discipline has developed many of the trappings of traditional academic disciplines. The *Indigenous Nations Studies Journal*, published by the Indigenous Nations Studies program at the University of Kansas, the *American Indian Quarterly*, published by the University of Nebraska Press, the *American Indian Culture and Research*

Journal, published by the American Indian Research Center at the University of California at Los Angeles, and *Wicaso Sa Review*, published by the University of Minnesota Press, provide an outlet for scholarly research and creative activity by faculty and graduate students in Native American Studies programs and in other academic programs throughout the country. *Ethnohistory*, the journal of the American Society for Ethnohistory, also provides a venue for scholarship on Native Americans.

CONCLUSION

Although a number of Native American Studies programs have disappeared since the 1970s, the number that have persisted and continue to flourish is evidence of the maturation of the field. Students majoring in such programs have gone on to successful careers in teaching, in professional areas such as law, social work, public administration, and other graduate programs, and in some cases to doctorates, either in Native American Studies at the two Universities that offer these programs (the University of Arizona and the University of California at Davis) or in disciplines at other universities.

The scholarship that has come out of these programs, and the interest in Native American scholarship by scholars in academic areas such as history, anthropology, literature, art, art history, and law has enriched the curricula of college and universities throughout the country. Native American Studies programs at the undergraduate level generally follow a liberal arts model of interdisciplinary study drawn from several departments, while at the graduate level, dedicated faculty resources in some cases or interdisciplinary committees administer programs that enable students to apply the kinds of new premises that we suggest in this book. What seems clear is that Native American Studies/American Indian Studies is becoming established in academic institutions as a field in its own right, and that the momentum of the scholarship will assure its continued existence.

NOTES

1. Frank C. Miller, 'Involvement in an urban university,' in *The American Indian in Urban Society*, ed. Jack O. Waddell and O. Michael Watson (Boston: Little, Brown and Company, 1971), pp. 312–40; Patricia Locke, *A Survey of College and University Programs for American Indians* (Boulder: Western Interstate Commission for Higher Education, 1978); Duane Champagne and Jay H. Stauss, *Native American Studies in*

Higher Education: Models for Collaboration between Universities and Indigenous Nations (Walnut Creek, CA: AltaMira Press, 2002).

2. Susan Guyette and Charlotte Heth, *Issues for the Future of American Indian Studies: A Needs Assessment and Program Guide* (Los Angeles: American Indian Studies Center, University of California, 1985).

3. *One-third of a Nation* ([Washington]: American Council on Education, in association with the Education Commission of the States, 1988).

4. Peter Novick, *That Noble Dream: The 'Objectivity Question' and the American Historical Profession* (Cambridge: Cambridge University Press, 1988).

5. Eva Marie Garroutte, *Real Indians: Identity and the Survival of Native America* (Berkeley: University of California Press, 2003); Joane Nagel, *American Indian Ethnic Renewal: Red Power and the Resurgence of Identity and Culture* (New York: Oxford University Press, 1996); Circe Sturm, *Blood Politics: Race, Culture and Identity in the Cherokee Nation of Oklahoma* (Berkeley: University of California Press, 2002).

6. Walter L. Williams, *The Spirit and the Flesh: Sexual Diversity in American Indian Culture* (Boston: Beacon Press, 1986); Sue-Ellen Jacobs, Wesley Thomas, Sabin Lang (eds), *Two-Spirit People: Native American Gender Identity, Sexuality, and Spirituality* (Urbana: University of Illinois Press, 1997); Will Roscoe, *The Zuni Man-Woman* (Albuquerque: University of New Mexico Press, 1991).

7. Theda Perdue, *Cherokee Women: Gender and Culture Change, 1700–1835* (Lincoln: University of Nebraska Press, 1998); Nancy Shoemaker (ed.), *Negotiators of Change: Historical Perspectives on Native American Women* (New York: Routledge, 1995); Patricia Albers and Beatrice Medicine (eds), *The Hidden Half: Studies of Plains Indian Women* (Lanham, MD: University Press of America, 1983); June Namias, *White Captives: Gender and Ethnicity on the American Frontier* (Chapel Hill: University of North Carolina Press, 1993).

8. Alvin M. Josephy, *America in 1492: The World of the Indian Peoples Before the Arrival of Columbus* (New York: Knopf Publishers, 1992); Donald L. Fixico, *Rethinking American Indian History* (Albuquerque: University of New Mexico Press, 1997); Devon A. Mihesuah, *Natives and Academics: Researching and Writing About American Indians* (Lincoln: University of Nebraska Press, 1998); Richard A. Grounds, George E. Tinker, and David Wilkins, *Native Voices: American Indian Identity and Resistance* (Lawrence: University of Kansas Press, 2003); Nancy Shoemaker, *Clearing a Path: Theorizing the Past in Native American Studies* (New York: Routledge Press, 2002); Russell Thornton, *Studying Native America: Problems and Prospects* (Madison: University of Wisconsin Press, 1998).

9. Robert A. Warrior, *Tribal Secrets: Recovering American Indian Intellectual Traditions* (Minneapolis: University of Minnesota Press, 1994); Jace Weaver, *That the People Might Live: Native American Literatures and Native American Community* (New York: Oxford University Press, 1997).

10. Elizabeth Cook-Lynn, *Anti-Indianism in Modern America: A Voice From Tatekeya's Earth* (Urbana: University of Illinois Press, 2001).

Suggestions for Further Reading

Any bibliography, by its very nature, becomes out of date even as it is being compiled. The following suggestions, in addition to the works in individual chapter notes, are not meant to constitute a canon but simply to suggest the range and variety of works on American Indians that have both shaped the field of Native American/American Indian studies and represent the innovative approaches that scholars have taken. Classic works such as Robert Berkhofer's *The White Man's Indian*, and Roy Harvey Pearce's *Savagism and Civilization* demonstrate how white American attitudes toward Indians tell us more about American values than they do about Indians, and they help us understand the sources of cultural conflict. Philip Deloria's *Playing Indian* gives that theme a new twist by arguing that Americans needed Indians to develop their own sense of a uniquely American identity.

Vine Deloria, Jr has been one of the most powerful and consistent critics of American attitudes toward Indians and one of the strongest proponents for the value of land as a source of religious identity. The essays collected in *For This Land* touch on the major themes of the second chapter of this book. Oscar Kawagley presents a very personal perspective on the traditional values of his own Yupiaq culture.

Historians have been writing about American Indians for a very long time, and the literature in this field is voluminous. One important and relatively early work, Alfred Crosby's *The Columbian Exchange*, inspired studies of 'the biological and cultural consequences of 1492' (the subtitle of the book) and demonstrated in a compelling way the impact of diseases on native populations. Neal Salisbury dealt with the cultural views that colored the perceptions of Indians and Europeans in early contact situations in New England, including the responses of Native people to the new material culture to which Europeans introduced them. As Native American history has evolved, more recent works such as Claudio Saunt's *A New Order of Things* and James Brooks's *Captives and Cousins* have dealt with cultural changes within Native societies, and R. Warren Metcalf's *Termination's Legacy: The Discarded Indians of Utah* and Alexandra Harmon's *Indians in the Making: Ethnic Relations and Indian Identities Around Puget Sound* have dealt with changing senses of Indian identity.

The concept of tribal sovereignty we describe as a 'moving target' that is being continually reinterpreted and renegotiated in relationships between Native nations and the federal and state governments. Although the book has been controversial among Native scholars, Fergus Bordewich's *Killing the White Man's Indian* presents a series of case studies that bring attention to the problems created by clashing definitions of the concept. The range of issues that we subsume under tribal sovereignty is large – economic development (Cornell and Kalt), Gaming (Mullis and Kamper), and repatriation (Mihesuah), to name only a few. Especially helpful in sorting out the legal issues involved in tribal sovereignty is David E. Wilkins and K. Tsianina Lomawaima, *Uneven Ground: American Indian Sovereignty and Federal Law.*

The literature on Native American languages is generally technical, but Keith Basso and Leanne Hinton are linguists who write about the cultural meanings of language as much as its structures. Alan Kilpatrick's *The Night Has a Naked Soul* introduces the reader to the complexity of language when used in highly sacred forms. Lyle Campbell's *American Indian Languages* is included because, although technical in its discussion of historical relationships among language groups, it allows the reader some grasp of the complexity of those relationships.

The critical study of American Indian literature begins with Paula Gunn Allen's aptly named edited collection, *Studies in American Indian Literature*, which came out of a National Endowment for the Humanities seminar that Dr Allen directed in 1977. It contains critical essays, course outlines, and bibliographies. Craig Womack, in *Red on Red*, has furthered the study of explicitly nationalistic Native literatures, that is, those that arise out of a specific tribal cultural sensibility and an internal form of criticism. Greg Sarris, in *Keeping Slug Woman Alive*, describes the interplay between the critic and the text/subject (individual author or storyteller). He argues that the critic cannot, in a study of Native texts, stand apart from the storyteller but must be engaged in a constant dialogue that creates the critical work out of cultural values. Gerald Vizenor's *Narrative Chance* is the ultimate dissection of traditional literary criticism in favor of the post-modern stance that he describes as 'survivance.'

The development of the field of American Indian art is beautifully portrayed in Margaret Archuleta's and Rennard Strickland's *Shared Visions: Native American Painters and Sculptors in the Twentieth Century*. Written as a catalogue for an exhibit mounted by the National Museum of the American Indian (NMAI) in 1993 in Washington, DC, it drew on Strickland's personal collection, and his status as a leading authority on American Indian art gives the book special value. Another NMAI publication, *This Path We Travel*, documents the travels of a group of fifteen contemporary artists to create the powerful multimedia exhibit (faux environments, video, and installments) that was one of the three opening exhibits mounted by NMAI at the opening of the George Gustav Heye Center in New York City in 1994. Lucy Lippard's *Partial Recall* critiques photography by and about Native Americans, and Beverly Singer's *Wiping the War Paint off the Lens* discusses Native Americans as film makers and videographers.

The final section of our list includes resources both for scholars and for new students of Native American Studies. It deals with sources of information, from very general encyclopedias and reference works to specialized bibliographies. The first works listed, by Haas, *Indians of North America: Methods and Sources for Library Research*, Hill, *Guide to Records* and *The Office of Indian Affairs*, and Hirschfelder et al. – although dated, are still useful tools. Haas deals with the organizational scheme used by libraries to classify American Indian materials, and Hirschfelder et al. provide an annotated list of materials. Phillip White's *American Indian Studies: A Bibliographic Guide* provides full annotations for most of the reference works that we cite in this bibliography. No serious researcher of Native American history could survive in the National Archives without Hill's indispensable guides to records concerning American Indians.

The *Handbook of North American Indians* is intended to be the definitive compilation of scholarly ethnographic information on the topic. Originally projected as a twenty-volume set to be produced in the early 1970s, its separate volumes, arranged by geographical areas with topical volumes on Indian-white relations, contemporary affairs, and languages, have emerged slowly over the years. The earliest, the northeast and southwest volumes, are now dated, although still valuable. The articles, maps and extensive bibliographies are certainly invaluable introductions to the ethnographic study of Native groups.

Charles Kappler's *Indian Affairs: Laws and Treaties* is the definitive compilation of the treaties signed by Indian tribes and ratified by the United States Senate from 1786 to 1871, and subsequent executive orders and acts of Congress through 1938 affecting Indian tribes. It is supplemented by Vine Deloria, Jr, and Raymond J. DeMallie in *Documents of American Indian Diplomacy*, which includes treaties with colonial governments, unratified treaties, treaties with the Confederacy, and other documents and orders affecting American Indian tribes. Charles Royce's *Indian Land Cessions* was originally published as part of the eighteenth annual report of the Bureau of American Ethnographic and is still considered the definitive source of maps depicting the boundaries of tribal land holdings and cessions as described in treaties.

The various bibliographies, encyclopedias and dictionaries will provide a guide to both factual information and the voluminous literature that supports Native American Studies. Bibliographies on individual tribes and certain topics can be found in the series published by the University of Indiana Press for the D'Arcy McNickle Center for the History of the American Indian at the Newberry Library in Chicago in the 1970s and 1980s and in the on-going series published by Scarecrow Press.

The journals described in the text are sources for the most current scholarship being done in the field of Native American Studies.

Some of the basic resources mentioned above, such as Royce's land cession maps and Kappler's treaties, are available through various Internet sites. A number of tribes have websites that include bibliographic information, but as with all websites, they should be used with caution.

CHAPTER I INTRODUCTION

Berkhofer, Robert F., *The White Man's Indian: Images of the American Indian from Columbus to the Present* (New York: Knopf, 1978).

Deloria, Philip J., *Playing Indian* (New Haven: Yale University Press, 1998).

Liberty, Margot, *American Indian Intellectuals of the Nineteenth and Early Twentieth Centuries* (Norman: Red River Books/University of Oklahoma Press, 2002).

Pearce, Roy Harvey, *Savagism and Civilization: A Study of the Indian and the American Mind* (Baltimore: Johns Hopkins Press, 1953).

Warrior, Robert Allen, *Tribal Secrets: Recovering American Indian Intellectual Traditions* (Minneapolis: University of Minnesota Press, 1994).

Zimmerman, Larry and Biolsi, Thomas (eds), *Indians and Anthropologists: Vine Deloria, Jr., and the Critique of Anthropology* (Tucson: University of Arizona Press, 1997).

CHAPTER 2 LAND AND IDENTITY

Deloria, Vine, Jr, *For This Land: Writings on Religion in America*, ed. James Treat (New York: Routledge, 1999).

Kawagley, Oscar, *A Yupiaq World View: A Pathway to Ecology and Spirit* (Prospect Heights, IL: Waveland Press, 1995).

Luckert, Karl, *The Navajo Hunter Tradition* (Tucson: University of Arizona Press, 1975).

Trigger, Bruce G., *The Children of Aataentic: A History of the Huron People to 1660* (Montreal: McGill-Queen's University Press, 1976).

Weaver, Jace, *Defending Mother Earth: North American Perspectives on Environmental Justice* (Maryknoll, NY: Orbis Books, 1996).

CHAPTER 3 HISTORICAL CONTACT AND CONFLICT

Brooks, James, *Captives and Cousins: Slavery, Kinship, and Community in the Southwest Borderlands* (Chapel Hill, NC: Omohundro Institute of Early American History and Cultures; Williamsburg, VA: University of North Carolina Press, 2002).

Calloway, Colin G., *One Vast Winter Count: The Native American West before Lewis and Clark* (Lincoln: University of Nebraska Press, 2003).

Cayton, Andrew R. L. and Teute, Fredrika, *Contact Points: American Frontiers from the Mohawk Valley to the Mississippi, 1750–1830* (Chapel Hill: University of North Carolina Press for the Institute of Early American History and Culture, 1998).

Crosby, Alfred W., *The Columbian Exchange: Biological and Cultural Consequences of 1492* (Westport, CT: Greenwood Publishing Co., 1972).

Deloria, Vine, Jr, and Wildcat, Daniel R., *Power and Place: Indian Education in America* (Golden, CO: Fulcrum Resources, 2001).

Eagle, Adam Fortunate, *Heart of the Rock: The Indian Invasion of Alcatraz* (Norman: University of Oklahoma Press, 2002).

Harmon, Alexandra, *Indians in the Making: Ethnic Relations and Indian Identities Around Puget Sound* (Berkeley: University of California Press, 1998).

Lobo, Susan and Peters, Kurt, *American Indians and the Urban Experience* (Walnut Creek: AltaMira Press, 2001).

Metcalf, R. Warren, *Termination's Legacy: The Discarded Indians of Utah* (Lincoln: University of Nebraska Press, 2002).

Miller, Susan A., *Coacoochee's Bones: A Seminole Saga* (Lawrence: University Press of Kansas, 2003).

Salisbury, Neal, *Manitou and Providence: Indians, Europeans and the Making of New England, 1500–1643* (New York: Oxford University Press, 1982).

Saunt, Claudio, *A New Order of Things: Property, Power, and the Transformation of the Creek Indians, 1733–1816* (Cambridge and New York: Cambridge University Press, 1999).

Sleeper-Smith, Susan, *Indian Women and French Men: Rethinking Cultural Encounter in the Western Great Lakes* (Amherst: University of Massachusetts Press, 2001).

Treat, James, *Around the Sacred Fire: Native Religious Activism in the Red Power Era: A Narrative Map of the Indian Ecumenical Conference* (Basingstoke: Palgrave McMillan, 2003).

CHAPTER 4 TRIBAL SOVEREIGNTY

Bordewich, Fergus, *Killing the White Man's Indian: Reinventing Native Americans at the End of the Twentieth Century* (New York: Doubleday, 1996).

Cornell, Stephen and Kalt, Joseph P., *What Can Tribes Do: Strategies and Institutions in American Indian Economic Development* (Los Angeles: American Indian Studies Center, University of California at Los Angeles, 1992).

Fowler, Loretta, *Tribal Sovereignty and the Historical Imagination: Cheyenne Arapaho Politics* (Lincoln: University of Nebraska Press, 2002).

Gonzalez, Mario and Cook-Lynn, Elizabeth, *The Politics of Hallowed Ground: Wounded Knee and the Struggle for Indian Sovereignty* (Urbana: University of Illinois Press, 1999).

Mihesuah, Devon (ed.), *A Repatriation Reader: Who Owns American Indian Remains?* (Lincoln: University of Nebraska Press, 2000).

Mullis, Angela and Kamper, David (eds), *Indian Gaming: Who Wins?* (Los Angeles: University of California at Los Angeles, American Indian Studies Center, 2000).

Norgren, Jill, *The Cherokee Cases: The Confrontation of Law and Politics* (New York: McGraw-Hill, 1996).

Thomas, David Hurst, *Skull Wars: Kennewick Man, Archaeology, and the Battle for Native American Identity* (New York: Basic Books, 2000).

Wilkins, David E., *American Indian Politics and the American Political System* (Lanham, MD: Rowman & Littlefield, 2002).

Wilkins, David E. and Lomawaima, K. Tsianina, *Uneven Ground: American Indian Sovereignty and Federal Law* (Norman: University of Oklahoma Press, 2001).

Williams, Robert A., Jr, *The American Indian in Western Legal Thought: The Discourses of Conquest* (New York: Oxford University Press, 1990).

Williams, Robert A., Jr, *Linking Arms Together: American Indian Treaty Visions of Law and Peace, 1600–1800* (New York: Oxford University Press, 1997).

CHAPTER 5 LANGUAGE

Basso, Keith, *Portraits of 'The Whiteman': Linguistic Play and Cultural Symbols Among the Western Apache* (Cambridge and New York: Cambridge University Press, 1979).

Basso, Keith, *Western Apache Language and Culture: Essays in Linguistic Anthropology* (Tucson: University of Arizona Press, 1990).

Campbell, Lyle, *American Indian Languages: The Historical Linguistics of Native America* (New York: Oxford University Press, 1997).

Hinton, Leanne, *Flutes of Fire: Essays on California Indian Languages* (Berkeley: Heyday Books, 1994).

Kilpatrick, Alan, *The Night has a Naked Soul: Witchcraft and Sorcery among the Western Cherokee* (Syracuse, NY: Syracuse University Press, 1997).

CHAPTER 6 INDIAN AESTHETICS: LITERATURE

Allen, Paula Gunn, *Studies in American Indian Literature* (New York: Modern Language Association, 1983).

Cook-Lynn, Elizabeth, *Why I Can't Read Wallace Stegner and Other Essays: A Tribal Voice* (Madison: University of Wisconsin Press, 1996).

Lincoln, Kenneth, *Native American Renaissance* (Berkeley: University of California Press, 1983).

Owens, Louis, *Other Destinies: Understanding the American Indian Novel* (Norman: University of Oklahoma Press, 1992).

Ruoff, La Vonne Brown, *American Indian Literatures: An Introduction, Bibliographic Review, and Selected Bibliography* (New York: Modern Language Association, 1990).

Ruppert, James, *Mediation in Contemporary Native American Fiction* (Norman: University of Oklahoma Press, 1995).

Sarris, Greg, *Keeping Slug Woman Alive: A Holistic Approach to American Indian Texts* (Berkeley: University of California Press, 1993).

Velie, Alan R., *Four American Indian Literary Masters* (Norman: University of Oklahoma Press, 1982).

Vizenor, Gerald, *Narrative Chance: Postmodern Discourse on Native American Indian Literatures* (Albuquerque: University of New Mexico Press, 1989).

Weaver, Jace, *That the People Might Live: Native American Literatures and Native American Community* (Oxford and New York: Oxford University Press, 1997).

Womack, Craig, *Red on Red: Native American Literary Separatism* (Minneapolis: University of Minnesota Press, 1999).

CHAPTER 7 INDIAN AESTHETICS: ART/EXPRESSIVE CULTURE

Archuleta, Margaret and Strickland, Rennard, *Shared Visions: Native American Painters and Sculptors in the Twentieth Century* (New York: New Press, 1991).

Berlo, Janet C. and Phillips, Ruth B., *Native North American Art* (Oxford: Oxford University Press, 1998).

Hill, Sarah H., *Weaving New Worlds: Southeastern Cherokee Women and their Basketry* (Chapel Hill: University of North Carolina Press, 1997).

Hill, Tom and Hill, Richard W., Sr, *Creation's Journey: Native American Identity and Belief* (Washington: Smithsonian Institution Press in collaboration with the National Museum of the American Indian, 1994).

Laubin, Reginald and Laubin, Gladys, *Indian Dances of North America: Their Importance to Indian Life* (Norman: University of Oklahoma Press, 1977).

Leuthold, Steven, *Indigenous Aesthetics: Native Art, Media, and Identity* (Austin: University of Texas Press, 1998).

Lippard, Lucy (ed.), *Partial Recall* (New York: New Press, 1992).

Rushing, W. Jackson, III (ed.), *Native American Art in the Twentieth Century* (London: Routledge, 1999).

Singer, Beverly R., *Wiping the War Paint off the Lens: Native American Film and Video* (Minneapolis: University of Minnesota Press, 2001).

This Path We Travel: Celebrations of Contemporary Native American Creativity (Washington, DC: National Museum of the American Indian, 1994).

GUIDES TO RESEARCH MATERIALS AND METHODS

Haas, Marilyn, *Indians of North America: Methods and Sources for Library Research* (Hamden, CT: Library Professional Publications, 1983).

Hill, Edward E., *Guide to Records in the National Archives of the United States Relating To American Indians* (Washington, DC: National Archives and Records Service, General Services Administration, 1981).

Hill, Edward E. *The Office of Indian Affairs, 1824–1880: Historical Sketches* (New York: Clearwater Publishing Company, Inc., 1974).

Hirschfelder, Arlene B., Byler, Mary Glover and Dorris, Michael A, *Guide to Research on North American Indians* (Chicago: American Library Association, 1983).

White, Phillip M., *American Indian Studies: A Bibliographic Guide* (Englewood, CO: Libraries Unlimited, 1995).

COMPILATIONS OF INFORMATION

Deloria, Vine, Jr and DeMallie, Raymond J., *Documents of American Indian Diplomacy: Treaties, Agreements and Conventions, 1775–1979*, 2 vols (Norman: University of Oklahoma Press, 1999).

Kappler, Charles J. (ed.), *Indian Affairs: Laws and Treaties*, 5 vols (Washington: Government Printing Office, 1904–41).

Prucha, Francis Paul (ed.), *Documents of United States Indian Policy*, 2nd edn (Lincoln: University of Nebraska Press, 1989).

Reddy, Marlita A. (ed.), *Statistical Record of Native North Americans* (Detroit, Washington, London: Gale Research Inc., 1993).

Royce, Charles C., *Indian Land Cessions in the United States* (Washington: Government Printing Office, 1899).

Sturtevant, William (general ed.), *Handbook of North American Indians*, 17 vols (Washington, DC: Smithsonian Institution, 1973–).

Tiller, Veronica E. Velarde, *American Indian Reservations and Trust Areas* (Washington: US Department of Commerce, Economic Development Administration, 1996).

Trigger, Bruce G., and Washburn, Wilcomb E., *The Cambridge History of the Native*

Peoples of the Americas, vol. I: North America (Cambridge: Cambridge University Press, 1996).

GENERAL REFERENCE WORKS

Champagne, Duane (ed.), *Native America: Portrait of the People* (Detroit: Visible Ink Press, 1994).

Champagne, Duane (ed.), *The Native North American Almanac: A Reference Work on Native North Americans in the United States and Canada* (Detroit: Gale Research, 1994).

Davis, Mary B. (ed.), *Native America in the Twentieth Century: An Encyclopedia* (New York: Garland, 1994).

Hirschfelder, Arlene B. and de Montano, Martha Kreipe, *The Native American Almanac: A Portrait of Native America Today* (New York: Prentice Hall General Reference, 1993).

Hoxie, Frederick E., *Encyclopedia of North American Indians* (Boston, New York: Houghton Mifflin, 1996).

Klein, Barry T., *Reference Encyclopedia of the American Indian*, 7th edn (West Nyack, NY: Todd Publications, 1995).

Markowitz, Harvey (consulting ed.), *American Indians*, 3 vols (Pasadena, CA: Salem Press, 1995).

Pritzker, Barry M. (ed.), *A Native American Encyclopedia: History, Culture, and Peoples* (New York: Oxford University Press, 2000).

SPECIALIZED REFERENCE WORKS

Bataille, Gretchen M. (ed.), *Native American Women: A Biographical Dictionary* (New York: Garland, 1993).

Crawford, Suzanne J. et al. (eds), *American Indian Religious Traditions: An Encyclopedia* (Santa Barbara: ABC-CLIO, 2004).

Deloria, Philip J. and Salisbury, Neal, *A Companion to American Indian History* (Malden, MA: Blackwell Publishers, 2001).

Gill, Sam D. and Sullivan, Irene F., *Dictionary of Native American Mythology* (Santa Barbara: ABC Clio, 1992).

Hirschfelder, Arlene B. and Molin, Paulette, *The Encyclopedia of Native American Religions: An Introduction* (New York: Facts on File, 1992).

Lester, Patrick D., *The Biographical Dictionary of American Indian Painters* (Tulsa: Servant Educational and Research Foundation, 1995).

Paterek, Josephine, *Encyclopedia of American Indian Costume* (Denver: ABC-Clio, 1994).

Waldman, Carl, *Who was Who in Native American History: Indians and Non-Indians from Early Contacts Through 1990* (New York: Facts on File, 1990).

Wiget, Andrew (ed.), *Dictionary of American Indian Literature* (New York: Garland, 1994).

BIBLIOGRAPHIES

Barrow, Mark V. et al., *Health and Disease of American Indians North of Mexico: a Bibliography* (Gainsville: University of Florida Press, 1972).

Bataille, Gretchen M. and Sands, Kathleen (eds), *American Indian Women: A Guide to Research* (New York: Garland, 1991).

Brumble, H. David, III, *An Annotated Bibliography of American Indian and Eskimo Autobiographies* (Lincoln: University of Nebraska Press, 1981).

Clements, William M. and Malpezzi, Frances M., *Native American Folklore, 1879–1979: An Annotated Bibliography* (Athens, OH: Swallow Press, 1984).

Danky, James Philip, ed., *Native American Periodicals and Newspapers, 1828–1982: Bibliography, Publishing Records and Holdings* (Westport, CT: Greenwood Press, 1984).

Green, Rayna, *Native American Women: A Contextual Bibliography* (Bloomington: Indiana University Press, 1983).

Haywood, Charles, *Bibliography of North American Folklore and Folksong*, vol. 2, *North American Indians* (New York: Dover Publications, 1961).

Hirschfelder, Arlene, *American Indian and Eskimo Authors* (New York: Association on American Indian Affairs, 1973).

Hoxie, Frederick E. and Markowitz, Harvey, *Native Americans: An Annotated Bibliography* (Pasadena, CA: Salem Press, 1991).

Kelso, Dianne R. and Attneave, Carolyn L., *Bibliography of North American Indian Mental Health* (Westport, CT: Greenwood Press, 1981).

Littlefield, Daniel F., Jr and Parins, James W., *A Biobibliography of Native American Writers, 1772–1924* (Metuchen, NJ: Scarecrow Press, 1981, Supplement 1985).

Littlefield, Daniel F., Jr, and Parins, James W., *American Indian and Alaska Native Newspapers and Periodicals*, 3 vols (Westport, CT: Greenwood Press, 1983–6).

Miller, Jay, Calloway, Colin G., and Sattler, Richard A., *Writings in Indian History, 1985–1990* (Norman: University of Oklahoma Press, 1995).

Moerman, Daniel, *American Medical Ethnobotany: A Reference Dictionary* (New York: Garland Publishing Co., 1977).

Murdock, George P. and O'Leary, T. J. (eds), *Ethnographic Bibliography of North America*, 4th edn, 5 vols (New Haven: Human Relations Area Files, 1975).

Owens, Mitchell V., *Bibliography of Health Issues Affecting North American Indians, Eskimos, and Aleuts 1950–1988* (Department of Health and Human Services, Public Health Service, Indian Health Service).

Prucha, Francis Paul, *A Bibliographical Guide to the History of Indian-White Relations in the United States* (Chicago: University of Chicago Press, 1977).

Prucha, Francis Paul, *Indian-White Relations in the United States: A Bibliography of Works Published 1975–1980* (Lincoln: University of Nebraska Press, 1982).

Sturtevant, William C., *Bibliography on American Indian Medicine and Health* (Washington: Smithsonian Institution, Bureau of American Ethnology, 1962).

Thornton, Russell and Grasmick, Mary K., *Bibliography of Social Science Research and Writings on American Indians* (Minneapolis: Center for Urban and Regional Affairs, University of Minnesota, 1979).

ATLASES

Murdock, George, *Ethnographic Atlas* (Pittsburgh: University of Pittsburgh Press, 1967).

Prucha, Francis Paul, *Atlas of American Indian Affairs* (Lincoln: University of Nebraska Press, 1990).

Tanner, Helen H., *Atlas of Great Lakes Indian History* (Norman: published for the Newberry Library by the University of Oklahoma Press, 1987).

Waldman, Carl, *Atlas of the North American Indian* (New York: Facts on File, 1985).

Index